# NOTES ON MENDELS:

# NOTES ON MENDELSSOHN

20 Crucial Works

Conrad Wilson

William B. Eerdmans Publishing Company
Grand Rapids, Michigan

*In memory of Leonard Friedman, founder of Mendelssohn on Mull and a passionate performer of Mendelssohn's music.*

First published 2005 by
SAINT ANDREW PRESS
Edinburgh

This edition published 2005
in the United States of America by
Wm. B. Eerdmans Publishing Company
255 Jefferson Ave. S.E., Grand Rapids, Michigan 49503

Printed in the United States of America

10 09 08 07 06 05    7 6 5 4 3 2 1

ISBN-10: 0-8028-2995-3
ISBN-13: 978-0-8028-2995-5

www.eerdmans.com

# CONTENTS

# FOREWORD

Why twenty? Obviously it is a device, one way of drawing attention to some of the masterpieces in a great composer's output. But at the same time it is a discipline and a challenge. Why choose these particular works and not others? The question and its answers are my reason for writing this book and its companions on other composers. In making my selection, I thought twenty works to be a good, sufficiently tight number. Increase it to thirty and choice becomes easier, perhaps too easy. Reduce it to ten and, in the case of great productive composers, you don't really have enough music wholly to justify what you are doing. Too many crucial works would have to be excluded, and the gaps would be glaring. So twenty it is, though not in the sense of a top twenty, because a crucial work does not actually have to be a great one, and the works are not listed – how could they be? – in any order of merit.

But each of them, it seems to me, needs to mark a special moment in its composer's life – perhaps a turning point, perhaps a sudden flash of inspiration, perhaps an intensifying of genius, as when Schubert produced his setting of Goethe's 'Gretchen am Spinnrade' at the age of 17, or Mozart his G major Violin Concerto, K216, at 19, or Beethoven his C minor Piano Trio, Op. 1, No. 3, at 25.

Yet none of these composers was a prodigy as gifted as Mendelssohn, whose String Octet and whose *A Midsummer Night's Dream* overture were the most astounding teenage masterpieces of all time. But if there was nothing so arresting to be found among Mozart's or Schubert's numerous boyhood works, the change when it came was startling.

With Schubert's first great song, Mozart's first great concerto and Beethoven's and Mendelssohn's first great pieces of chamber music came the shock of surprise in the form of an audacious new command of melody and accompaniment, a conspicuous leap in quality and, in the slow movement of the Mozart, a grasp of the mystery of beauty which made his two previous violin concertos, written in the same year, seem blandly impersonal exercises in composition.

Yet this third of Mozart's five violin concertos is not a masterpiece in the sense that *Don Giovanni* is, just as Schubert's boyhood String Quartet in E flat major, D87, for all its melodic beauty, is not as overwhelming as 'Death and the Maiden'. Nor, for that matter, does the fizz of Mendelssohn's early string symphonies have the passion of his A minor String Quartet, written very soon afterwards.

It is not the aim of these books to set one masterpiece against another, or to suggest that early works are automatically less interesting than late ones. To regard a composer's output purely as a process of evolution is to fail inexcusably to accept a work on its own terms – a serious flaw in assessments of Schubert, who, according to many a pundit, did not 'find' himself until he was almost dead. In Mendelssohn, the division between what is 'early' and what is 'late' and what is the difference between them becomes less and less clearly demarcated.

So, early works are not being banned from these pages, even if it means the loss of some late ones. Nor is my decision to deal with the music chronologically based on any intrinsic belief that it reflects in some special way a composer's progress. The intention is simply to shed light on what was happening to him at the time he wrote a particular piece, where he was, what he was doing or experiencing, and how the music fits into the general pattern of his life and output. To go beyond this, by claiming that Haydn, for example, 'progressed' from his *Storm and Stress* symphonies to his *London* ones, or Mozart from his E flat major Piano Concerto, K271, to his E flat major, K482, is to undervalue his achievement as a whole.

So, no masterpiece has been omitted simply because its composer later in some way surpassed it. Some works are included simply because I adore them, or am prepared to defend them against the judgement of people who detest them. Liking a piece of music, we should always remember, is not the opposite of disliking it. It is a different condition altogether, and being able to explain why we like it is perhaps more important in the end than pronouncing on whether it is good music or bad.

# NOTES ON MENDELSSOHN

Each of these twenty short essays is a species of what are traditionally known as programme notes — the descriptions to be found in printed concert or opera programmes of what is being performed that night. Donald Francis Tovey, one-time professor of music at Edinburgh University, was a famed and erudite pioneer of the form in the early twentieth century, and his collected *Essays in Musical Analysis* remain good to read, even if their style now seems old-fashioned and out of tune with today's musical thinking. Nor are they always accurate. Scholarship has progressed since Tovey's time.

Nevertheless, what Tovey wrote still towers over much of what passes for programme notes today. Even during my own post-Tovey boyhood, programme notes incorporated — as Tovey's did — musical examples because it was assumed that concert-goers could read music. Today, such notes would be branded elitist. To include musical terminology at all tends to be frowned upon. I have been asked why, in my own notes, I employ such terms as 'counterpoint', which nobody understands. But are football correspondents similarly chided for writing 'penalty' or 'free kick'? Somehow I think not. Though I am all against jargon, the use of an established, accessible musical term is preferable to a paragraph of explanation.

Concert programmes are now a dumbed-down art in which fatuous puffs about the performers occupy more space than the notes themselves, and adverts are given more space still. Traditional notes, as the chief executive of a concert organisation has remarked to me, are now 'irrelevant'. In the sense that most concerts today take place in darkened halls, he was perhaps right. But notes are written to be read before and after an event, as well as during it, and this book's intention is to fill that need.

In the sixteen years I spent editing the Edinburgh Festival's programme notes, there were a number of house rules which I worked out with the then Festival director, Peter Diamand, whose European outlook differed from, and was refreshingly less 'commercial' than, the British. Diamand's beliefs, which I shared, were that notes should contain facts rather than flimflam; that speculation was acceptable so long as it was informed; that notes should be coherently devised by a single writer for the contents of a single programme; that connections between one work and another should be mentioned; that the author, as Tovey once decreed, should act as counsel for the defence – Diamand detested notes which gave the impression that 'This is a bad work but let's perform it anyway'; and that artists' biographies should be confined to 150 words, should include no adjectives and should supply no information about what a performer would be performing in future seasons.

Though most of these principles have fallen by the wayside, they are still the ones to which I, as a note-writer, would prefer to adhere. In addition, I would say that, wherever possible, a work's place in musical history needs to be established; that its local connections (if any) should be mentioned; and that the writer has a responsibility to lure the reader into the music.

Some of the notes included in these pages are based on notes originally written for one musical organisation or another, but which have gone through a constant process of change, and which have now been changed yet again to suit the needs of a book about a single great composer. No note, whether for a concert programme or for something more permanent, should be merely 'drawn from stock'. Just as every performance of a work forms a part (however small) of that work's history, so every programme note should reflect the state – and status – of that work at the time the annotator is writing about it. Attitudes alter. Here, in this book, are twenty current attitudes (my own, but also quoting those of others) to twenty works that continue to matter.

Finally, a note on format. Each book begins with a fresh assessment of its subject composer and of the way he is performed at the start of the twenty-first century. Recordings are recommended at the end of each short essay. Books are listed for further reading, and technical terms are explained in a brief glossary.

CONRAD WILSON
*Edinburgh, 2005*

# INTRODUCTION

Mendelssohn's – like Purcell's, Mozart's, Schubert's and Chopin's – was a short life into which much was packed. Sometimes, in contemplating his multifarious other achievements, you marvel that he had time to compose at all. Yet compose he did, and in cornucopian abundance. His fecundity, however, was to prove his undoing. What began as genius – and Mendelssohn's genius at the age of 16, or even earlier, spoke for itself – diminished, or so it was said, at shocking speed into what came to be dismissed as enervating blandness. The absolute harmlessness of his later works was deemed a terrible warning to all creative artists who lead comfortable and seemingly saintly lives. Even *Elijah*, that most ambitious of oratorios, was wrecked by its milk-and-water harmonies.

Something the same, of course, has been said of Richard Strauss, who, having attained the ferocious dissonance of *Elektra*, stepped back from the brink and wrote *Der Rosenkavalier*. It was an act which prevented him, some would say, from ever becoming a great composer.

So why do we still listen to Strauss's later works? Why, more to the point, do we listen to Mendelssohn's? These include, after all, the 'Scotch' symphony (his at last acknowledged masterpiece in the form) and the lacerating but little-known final string quartet. The only possible explanation is that late Mendelssohn has been falsely maligned, that only some of the works suffer from blandness, and that, far from sliding into talented professionalism, his inspiration stayed intact and indeed gained a new intensity in the years immediately before his death.

Those who continue to claim otherwise – and there is a tradition even among acknowledged Mendelssohn authorities to be snooty about this sometimes snooty composer – are either not listening properly or else are lazily willing to accept stale, slovenly, handed-down opinions. To say you dislike Mendelssohn's music is one thing; to dismiss it as empty note-spinning is quite another.

Even the praise which Mendelssohn receives tends to be meted out grudgingly. Of his fine and powerful Piano Trio in D minor, it is said that he attempts to draw from his material 'a tragic weight it does not really have'. His First Piano Concerto is racy but empty, his Violin Concerto sleek and sentimental. But then, coming from the composer of 'Oh for the Wings of a Dove', what would you expect?

Alternatively known as 'Hear My Prayer', this ditty from *Saint Paul* laid the composer open to Bernard Shaw's accusation of 'despicable oratorio-mongering', its mawkishness amplified in 1927 by Master Ernest Lough's best-selling record whose soaring phrases seemed the very soul of treble-voiced sanctimony. Yet most great composers have their mongering moments – Mozart's morbid *Ave Verum Corpus* (which some choose to have sung at their weddings, others more appropriately at their funerals) is in its quiet way scarcely less cringe-inducing – and Mendelssohn has been rebuked for the sheer awfulness of 'Hear My Prayer' more often than he deserves. As the *Record Guide* rightly put it in the 1950s, he was much too fine a musician ever to deserve contempt.

Yet the question remains: how fine? Shaw, according to the composer's latest and excellent biographer, R. Larry Todd, 'reinforced a view of Mendelssohn as effeminate', with the visual support of Aubrey Beardsley, whose 1896 caricature of the composer showed him with rosebud lips, a bow tie round his neck, a quill in his left hand, and dainty shoes on his tiny feet.

But his Victorian admirers, accused of over-praising him, can now simply be seen to have focused on the wrong pieces for the wrong reasons. They doted on him, massaged his vanity and prompted him to feed their religiosity with a constant supply of new sacred works, which was the only sort of new music that mattered to them and which, in any case, he seemed happy to write. Later they did the same to Dvořák, whose nine visits to England helped to pay for his estate in southern Bohemia but saddled posterity with such atrocities as his Stabat Mater, his Requiem and his *St Ludmila* cantata, a work of infinite tedium unwisely revived for the closing concert of the 2002 Edinburgh Festival.

# NOTES ON MENDELSSOHN

Mendelssohn's contributions to the English Choral Tradition, which he was invariably invited to conduct in person, were not only exhaustingly time-consuming but also seriously damaged his health, sapping his energy just when he was entering what should have been his vital middle years. His correspondence of the period, with its increasing references to the need to cut back, to constant fatigue, to blinding headaches, is sadder to read in its way than Mozart's notorious begging letters, which tended, as we now realise, to be mere formalities during periods of overspending, whereas Mendelssohn's letters ring all too true. For all their musical fluency, both composers, of course, grossly overworked themselves and finally paid the penalty for it.

If Britain had demanded the right things of Mendelssohn — the sort of things Dvořák would later bestow on America — who knows how his career would have progressed? But the stroke which killed him at the age of 38 was clearly caused by the same congenital weakness as the one which killed his beloved sister Fanny a few months earlier. Though Fanny's death, and the strain of composing *Elijah*, may have speeded his demise, it seems unlikely that he would have survived much longer. His grandfather Moses had been felled at 56 by a stroke, as had his father Abraham at 59, prompting Fanny's all-too-accurate pronouncement: 'It was a beautiful, enviable end, and I pray to God for a similar death'. Her prayer was answered. She collapsed, aged 41, while rehearsing one of her brother's works.

To say that the Victorians destroyed Mendelssohn would be too severe. It would have happened anyway. But, if they had demanded more chamber music rather than church music, posterity would have had greater cause for gratitude. The last of his string quartets, his sister's death savagely engraved on every page, shows him to have been heading musically into a new and surely very different period of creativity.

Mendelssohn's rages, one of which prompted him to tear his score of Beethoven's *Egmont* in two during a rehearsal, are not much spoken of, perhaps because nobody associates them with so seemingly polite a person. But they were there, even if, unlike Schubert, he did not conspicuously transfer them to his music. In the case of the F minor Quartet, however, he did so, and the effect was shattering.

So the question keeps recurring. How great a composer was he or could he have been? Was he a great composer at all? Since many people would say no, the time is clearly ripe to reassess him. His post-Victorian fall from grace is long since over. Wagner's anti-semitic denouncement of him, which did not stop him filching some of Mendelssohn's ideas, was typically mean-spirited. Modern composers continue to patronise him – it would be hard to imagine Pierre Boulez conducting his music – yet his stock is conspicuously rising.

Lunching in Edinburgh some years ago with Alan Walker, professor of music at McMaster University in Hamilton, Ontario, I found myself lured into a game of 'the ten best' – a subject in which he was clearly well practised. All I had to do, he said, was compile a list of the ten greatest composers. He would do the same, and we would find ourselves in virtual agreement. As author of a fascinating study entitled *An Anatomy of Music Criticism*, in which he sought to lay a theoretical foundation for the making and explaining of value judgements, he spoke confidently enough to convince me that our views would not seriously diverge.

And in fact we differed on only one composer. Mendelssohn was on Walker's list but not on mine. Today we would be in complete agreement. It is not just that, in the American pianist Charles Rosen's words, Mendelssohn was 'the greatest child prodigy the history of Western music has ever known'. Nor is it, as the English critic Paul Driver has asserted, that he was at the time of his death perhaps the most widely revered musician in Europe, not only among the 'great composers' but also as a conductor did more than most to establish that canon. It is because he was the composer of works – the Octet for a start – whose greatness is sufficiently self-evident to require no explanation.

Yet it is the critic's task, or so we would claim, not only to hail greatness but to explain it. As Walker has pointed out, however, the greatness comes first. The explanation is what follows. It is as good a test as any, and it is one which, at the start of another century, Mendelssohn passes with ease.

Just as Offenbach was called the Mozart of the Champs-Elysées, Mendelssohn was known, more prosaically, as the Mozart of the nineteenth century. In each case, by implication, Mozart set a standard towards which others could only aspire. Why, then, mention him at all? If Mendelssohn was a great composer, it was due to his own inspiration and his own responses to the classical forms to which Mozart had responded also. But Mendelssohn's F minor String Quartet, Op. 80, is a masterpiece not because it was composed by the Mozart of the nineteenth century but because it was by Mendelssohn. Sometimes, for creative reasons of his own, he leaned towards Beethoven, and sometimes he leaned towards Bach, whose *St Matthew Passion* he rediscovered and popularised. But when Bach and Beethoven are audible in his music, they filter through his thought processes and emerge sounding more like Mendelssohn than themselves.

*Mendelssohn was born in Hamburg in 1809 but, as a Jew, was soon moved to what seemed the greater security of Berlin. His grandfather Moses was a distinguished philosopher. His father Abraham was a prosperous banker who abandoned Judaism and had his children baptised into Protestantism. But, a Christian Mendelssohn being considered a contradiction in terms, his name was hyphenated into Mendelssohn-Bartholdy, to nobody's particular pleasure, it would seem, though it is still sometimes written full-out by pedantic people.*

*Mendelssohn's elder sister Fanny played Bach's forty-eight preludes and fugues from memory at the age of 12, and could have developed, had she been encouraged,* into a composer of distinction. The fact that Mendelssohn passed some of her music off as his own has been held against him by modern feminists, but he doubtless thought it was the only way to get it performed at all. As a child, he wrote epic poems even earlier than Fanny played the forty-eight, and, on a visit to Goethe in Weimar, reported that he received kisses every morning 'from the author of Faust and Werther'. On holiday in Switzerland, he displayed flair as a watercolour painter. He was by then 13 and had already written his twelve symphonies for strings. His real career had begun.

# One

## 1823
## QUARTET NO. 2 IN F MINOR FOR PIANO AND STRINGS, OP. 2

Allegro molto                                              Adagio

Intermezzo: Allegro moderato                    Allegro molto vivace


By composing his stupendous Octet for strings at the age of 16, Mendelssohn declared his genius with a speed not even Mozart could match. In fact, he declared it long before he was 16. The first of his piano quartets, for instance, was written at 13, the second at 14 along with the first of his three string quartets in the key of E flat major, and his racy Piano Sextet (misleadingly numbered Op. 110) at 15.

The dozen-or-so symphonies for strings, music brimming with vivacity and audacity which was allowed to gather dust for 150 years, pre-dated all of these. Not one of them was a piece of juvenilia in the ordinary sense. Even to call them student works, which in one way they were, would be to demean them. Mendelssohn never went to school. Relying on private tutors for his education, he was clearly born to be a great composer and proved it, with no audible sense of boyhood struggle, by producing exemplary music in all the established forms of the period. To have heard him play the airy, nimble, polished piano parts in some of these pieces would have been a privilege – dare one say it? – even greater than hearing Mozart perform at the same age.

His teacher, Carl Zelter, must have sensed this when, in 1823, he told his precocious pupil that 'From this day you are no longer an apprentice but an independent member of the brotherhood of musicians. In the name of Mozart, Haydn, and old father Bach, I proclaim you independent.'

The words may now sound improbably theatrical, and carelessly omitted Beethoven, but there was no doubt about their message. Though Mendelssohn was never an apprentice in the ordinary sense, he was independent enough at the age of 14, when Zelter made his proclamation, to compose his F minor Piano Quartet with an aplomb that spoke forcefully for itself.

Listen to the first movement of this work, with its typically Mendelssohnian contrasts between minor-key poignancy and major-key sweetness, its mingling of poise and passion, and you will encounter in pristine form the essence of his style. The sudden surge of speed and intensity towards the end is as timely as it is exciting – how did a boy of such secluded upbringing think of it? – and the succeeding *adagio*, with its tenderly pulsating accompaniment, is a song without words in young

Felix's most felicitous vein. He may have done such things even better in later works; but here again, it should be noted, he shows his aptitude for finding the most appropriate of endings.

The next movement is even more amazing in its ability to show that Mendelssohn was already Mendelssohn at the age of 14. A fascinating forerunner of future movements of its kind, it accurately matches length to content at a speed too slow to make it sound like a scherzo but which perfectly fits Mendelssohn's specific choice of the term intermezzo. Brahms would later find the same title much to his taste, but it was Mendelssohn who paved the way with music of dancelike grace – flowing, gentle, succinct, plaintive – ideally suited to form one of the tightly structured middle movements of so many of his works. The finale, a species of *perpetuum mobile*, is a sustained juggling act of the sort he would perfect in his Octet; but here, already, his flair for giddy momentum is on exhilarating display.

Yet, for all its sureness of touch and beauty of expression, the work remains a rarity, almost wholly neglected by performers and record companies. You won't find any of today's celebrity pianists championing it, though at least it was heard in Manchester's revelatory festival of Mendelssohn's chamber music in 2002. For a recording, look no further than the budget-price Naxos company's Mendelssohn series, which includes a coupling of this work with the B minor Piano Quartet, Op. 3, by the aptly-named Bartholdy Piano Quartet (8.550967). The names of the players (German and Italian) may be unfamiliar, but the performances are warm, assured and well recorded in Heidelberg's Clara Wieck Auditorium.

The same can be said for a second disc, coupling the C minor Piano Quartet, Op. 1, with the D major Piano Sextet, Op. 110 – an entrancing work from almost the same period as Schubert's *Trout* quintet, employing almost the same forces. Why these flowery samples of early Schubert and even earlier Mendelssohn never appear side by side in the concert hall can only be because almost nobody knows the Mendelssohn. Here (on Naxos 8.550966) is a chance to discover its delights.

The substantial String Symphony No. 11 in F major, with its sombrely mysterious introduction, agitated *allegro molto* and songlike 'Swiss' scherzo, shows early Mendelssohnian fire spreading in a different direction. Along with four more of these works, it receives a performance on period instruments from the Concerto Köln, the first movement filled with storm and stress quite startling in its vehemence, the charm of the scherzo intruded upon by pounding kettledrums (Elatus 2564-60440-2).

# Two

## 1824
## SYMPHONY NO. 1 IN C MINOR, OP. 11

Allegro di molto          Andante

Menuetto: Allegro molto          Allegro con fuoco

Mendelssohn earned his reputation as a *wunderkind* principally through two teenage masterpieces, the Octet for Strings and the overture to *A Midsummer Night's Dream*, which seemed to erupt out of the happiest combination of circumstances – his benign family background, his beneficial boyhood travels, his brilliance as a pianist, his musical intelligence, his linguistic fluency, his inspirational elder sister who at the age of 14 was an expert exponent of Bach, and the fact that, by the time he himself was 14, he had his own private orchestra. Mozart could not have achieved more – and indeed, at that point in his life, had actually achieved less.

Yet the fizz of the Octet and the magic of the overture were not the first manifestations of Mendelssohn's astounding precocity. Before either of these works proclaimed his genius, he had composed, at 15, his scarcely less impressive Symphony No. 1, which would have been his Symphony No. 13 if he had not decided against bestowing numbers on the twelve by no means schoolboy symphonies for strings that preceded it. Why this work continues to be confined to the fringe of the repertoire, and patronised as just another piece of juvenilia, is a mystery. But if its neglect has an explanation (beyond the misfortune that it is the only full-scale Mendelssohn symphony to lack an invitingly descriptive title) it lies perhaps in the shortage of instantly memorable melodies with which his more popular works are plentifully endowed.

The point about Mendelssohn's Symphony No. 1, however, is that it is not primarily about melody. It is not even primarily about Mendelssohnian 'charm', though some commentators have professed to hear it that way. Its main ingredient is energy, which drives it from the first notes of the opening movement to the last notes of the finale with only the gentle slow movement and the middle section of the minuet providing brief points of repose. The theory that Mendelssohn was a limp, effeminate young man – who was reputedly chaperoned on to the platform 'like a young lady' for the premiere of this very symphony – is at odds with the surging vitality of the music. The first movement begins very much as it means to continue, with pounding rhythms, thudding kettledrums and the odd hint of Beethoven – even the choice of the key of C minor was a Beethovenian feature.

What is more remarkable, however, is that it all sounds so characteristically Mendelssohnian. Could it ever be mistaken for anyone else? Well, there is a chance suggestion of Schubert in some of the woodwind colouring, though Mendelssohn's renowned discovery of Schubert did not come until later. In fact, the woodwind influence more probably stemmed from Weber; but what is principally brought to mind by this fiery music is Mendelssohn's own *Ruy Blas* overture, a tribute to Victor Hugo written fifteen years later.

Tense and taut, the first movement does not slacken its grip until the soft arrival of the major-key andante, a lovely early example of Mendelssohn's flair for songs without words. The robust minuet is neither a courtly dance nor the sort of gossamer scherzo which would later become a Mendelssohn speciality. Its roots lie, if anywhere, in the equivalent movement of Mozart's Symphony No. 40, but the hymnlike central section is pure Mendelssohn. His decision to replace this movement, when he conducted the work in London, with an orchestration of the scherzo from the Octet for strings showed a surprising loss of faith in a fine piece of music.

If the Mozart connection is resumed quite startlingly at the beginning of the finale, the music soon proceeds to do very different things, one of which is to unfurl a romantically operatic but less Mozartian theme for clarinet and pizzicato strings. The subsequent fugue sounds not so much like the desperate inclusion of an academic device as a genuine intensification of the drama — and Mendelssohn, we should remember, wrote some of the best fugues after Bach. The triumphant swing to C major at the end is exhilarating, and all the better for sounding neither like a tribute to Beethoven's Fifth Symphony nor like a foretaste of Brahms's First.

Sadly neglected in the concert hall, Mendelssohn's First Symphony is similarly cold-shouldered by the record companies. To get your hands on it, you may find yourself having to buy not only the four other symphonies but several more Mendelssohn works as well. Claudio Abbado's strong, lithe performance with the London Symphony Orchestra comes in this lavish four-disc format (DG 415 353-2) but also, most opportunely, on a single disc along with the similarly neglected 'Reformation' symphony (DG 445 596-2). This is the coupling also favoured by Reinhard Seifried and the National Symphony Orchestra of Ireland, who are not to be shunned simply because they are less famous than Abbado and his London forces (Naxos 8.550957).

# Three

## 1825
## OCTET IN E FLAT MAJOR FOR STRINGS, OP. 20

Allegro moderato ma con fuoco                          Andante

Scherzo: Allegro leggierissimo                          Presto


No teenage work proclaims its composer's genius more conspicuously than Mendelssohn's Octet, whose youthful verve, brilliance and perfection make it one of the miracles of nineteenth-century music. How he came to write it remains a mystery. Not even Mozart at the age of 16 produced anything to rival its chutzpah. Its choice of instruments – four violins, two violas and two cellos – would have prompted another composer simply to write a scholarly 'double' string quartet, employing what we would today call stereophonic effects between the first group of strings and the second. Spohr's once fashionable octets of the same period were like that, employing the full body of strings only at points of climax.

But what Mendelssohn did was something infinitely more resourceful and integrated, as one twentieth-century Scottish-based composer, Kenneth Leighton, recognised when he was commissioned to write a work for the same forces that could share a programme with Mendelssohn's masterpiece during the Edinburgh Festival.

Determined to analyse exactly how Mendelssohn had done it, and to employ his research to his own purposes, he soon admitted defeat and wrote a different sort of octet altogether. Mendelssohn's piece, indeed, rejects forensic examination in the same way as does the Mona Lisa or the Piazza San Marco. The composer's personal background, pleasant as it was, provides no clue. He was the son of a wealthy Berlin banker. He was loved, well educated and encouraged to play the piano and violin. He learnt how to paint as well as compose. He was given money to travel. And in his teens he wrote not only his Octet but also, in the same burst of inspiration, the overture to *A Midsummer Night's Dream*. He was soon to be renowned in Leipzig as conductor of the great Gewandhaus Orchestra. At the age of 20, he discovered – and championed – Bach's *St Matthew Passion*. He became Queen Victoria's favourite composer. Though born a Jew, he became a Lutheran and composed a 'Reformation' symphony quoting Lutheran themes. Italy inspired his 'Italian' symphony and Scotland his 'Scotch'.

Yet the fairy who placed so many gifts at his disposal omitted the one which – or so posterity cruelly decreed – really mattered. She forgot to bestow on him the ability to mature in the way that Beethoven or Schubert or indeed Mozart did. What Mendelssohn wrote towards the end of his sadly short life was no better, it was claimed, than what he had written at the beginning. Some people, indeed, would claim that it was not so good. But that was simply sour grapes. Though he could be said to have peaked early – and the Octet, as we are gradually becoming aware, was not even his first work of genius – Mendelssohn did not slide downhill. He composed with ease and, as his opponents are increasingly unable to dispute, he quite often hit the jackpot. His late chamber music, in its way, was quite the equal of his early, and much less sedate than was once thought.

But his Octet remains a case apart, a masterpiece of an extraordinary and unrepeatable sort. From start to finish, it moves with power steering. The opening *allegro*, its main theme launched by the first violin over a range of three octaves, is an object lesson in how to make dynamic and passionate use of simple arpeggios, in which all eight instruments are instantly involved, all of them doing different things. As an instrumental tour de force there had been nothing like it, but the simple arpeggios on which so much of the first movement is based are less simple than they sound. The music, as it progresses, becomes more and more harmonically adventurous, without losing track of what have been called the great anchors of E flat major and B flat major on which the movement's entire structure is built.

The second movement is a comfortable minor-key *andante*, sweet and poignant, a model of its kind, which avoids slipping into sentimentality. The fleet, silvery scherzo, which in an inflated orchestral version used to be presented as a concert piece in its own right (as if the rest of the work were not worth playing), anticipates the gossamer atmosphere of *A Midsummer Night's Dream* and is required to be played pianissimo and staccato throughout, with the utmost lightness of touch ('leggierissimo'). As the composer's sister Fanny put it, the trills move with the speed of lightning, the music making you feel 'so near the world of spirits, carried away in the air, half inclined to snatch up a broomstick and follow the aerial procession'. Its inspiration, according to Mendelssohn himself, lay in the *Walpurgisnacht* dream in Goethe's *Faust*, to which he would later devote his *Erste Walpurgisnacht*, a masterpiece in which he came closer to Berliozian fantasy than in any other work, yet which even now remains reprehensibly neglected.

In the end, the scherzo vanishes with the flick of a magic wand; but Mendelssohn's incomparable sleight of hand instantly resumes in the finale. From the bottom of the register, the music begins to seethe with volcanic energy before erupting with twice the impetus of the preceding movement. A new theme emerges, built upon hammering unisons suggestive of the repeated anvil strokes in the finale of the Great C major Symphony which Schubert was writing almost simultaneously in Vienna – though neither composer knew what the other was doing.

Then, as the music develops, the strains of the scherzo suddenly return, so precisely woven into the texture that it seems not only a quotation of something already heard but a natural part of the finale. Though Beethoven, in the finale of his Fifth Symphony, had done something similar, it was for conspicuously dramatic reasons. Mendelssohn's aims were different; and, in achieving such perfection of integration, he invented the art of cyclic structure which would be enthusiastically adopted by other composers – Dvořák, Franck and Liszt, to name but three – as the nineteenth century progressed. Quite apart from that, however, the finale is one of the most ceaselessly joyous webs of counterpoint ever to have been spun.

The best performances of Mendelssohn's Octet come from players who adore the music and love working together. Whether they are members of the Vienna Philharmonic performing it in the Musikverein, or the British ensemble led by the violinists Leonard Friedman and Emanuel Hurwitz who launched the Mendelssohn on Mull Festival with a vibrant account of it in a village hall in the 1980s, is of secondary importance. It is the rapport that counts, and it is found, sadly, on very few discs, simply because a recording studio is no place for music such as this. But the Vienna Octet, its players drawn from the parent Philharmonic, seems thoroughly at ease in a recording made in the city's Sofiensaal in 1973, with Beethoven's Septet as the appropriate coupling (Decca 421093-2).

Those who find the sound a little dated may prefer the equally sympathetic performance by members of the Academy of St Martin-in-the-Fields. Again the recording is by no means new, but the ambience is warm and the coupling, Mendelssohn's fine String Quintet in B flat, Op. 87, even more apt (Philips 420 400-2PH).

# Four

Mendelssohn was a stripling of 17, but already an experienced composer and pianist, when he read Shakespeare's *A Midsummer Night's Dream* and was inspired to write a concert overture on the subject. It revealed him as even more precocious than Mozart, who at that age had produced nothing comparable. Yet Mendelssohn's was no sudden explosion of genius. The great Octet for strings had been composed a year earlier, the dozen-or-so delicious String Symphonies and the sophisticated Piano Sextet, Op. 110, earlier still, and the wrongly-numbered 'Reformation' symphony, long assumed to be a late work, was late only in the sense that he was 21 when he wrote it.

In hailing young Felix as 'the greatest child prodigy the history of Western music has ever known', the pianist and writer Charles Rosen was neither exaggerating nor inviting challenge. But those who dismiss Mendelssohn as a musical Peter Pan, destined never to mature, are on shakier ground. The theory that his genius operated on autopilot during the last years of his short life is equally weak, contradicted by the poetry of his 'Scotch' symphony (1842), the romance of his Violin Concerto (1844) and – unlike any other of his works – the desolation of his final String Quartet in F minor, Op. 80 (1847), written in memory of his beloved sister Fanny, from whose death he never recovered.

Yet the sheer resourcefulness of his teenage Shakespearian overture remains something to marvel at. Four soft, exquisitely spaced woodwind chords, mysterious and recurring, set the tone and mark the structure of the music. The fairies in fine-spun flight, the lovers in the forest, the braying of Bottom in his ass's head are all vividly present, portrayed with brilliance and finesse, Bottom's hee-haws being delivered by the now obsolete ophicleide, the tuba-like brass instrument, with keys rather than valves, favoured by Mendelssohn for this role. Caring conductors rightly make an effort to obtain an ophicleide, and a person who can play it, for performances of this work; lazier ones make do with a tuba.

The first performance was given in November 1827 without ophicleide, but without much else either. Mendelssohn not yet having orchestrated the overture, he and his sister Fanny played it as a piano duet to members of the family in their recently acquired Berlin abode at 3 Leipziger Strasse, a palace surrounded by its own private parkland. It was an area, close to the Potsdamer Platz, through which the Berlin Wall would later cut but by then the building had been demolished.

In Mendelssohn's day, the street experienced no such dramas – partly because the acres of pasture, with resident cows, usefully secluded the family from the anti-semitism already spreading through Berlin. The dramas in which the Marvellous Boy was himself involved were games of charades, civilised play-readings and domestic productions, including *A Midsummer Night's Dream*, an enlightened choice for a city in which Shakespeare was deemed a mediocrity.

Not until the overture had been played under these domestic conditions did Felix get down to orchestrating it, thereby inventing the shimmering sound-world now so recognisably associated with his music. The work received its full orchestral premiere a few months later in the Polish city of Stettin, which, with its long Jewish history, would suffer severely during the Holocaust. Britain first heard it on Midsummer's Eve 1829, soon after Mendelssohn's far-reaching revival of Bach's *St Matthew Passion* in Berlin, a performance grand but hardly authentic, with a chorus of 400 to give it the body that Mendelssohn considered it needed.

The fact that he could return to the subject of Shakespeare's comedy seventeen years later, as if the overture had been written only yesterday, has always been cited as proof of his Peter Pan-ishness. Had he really never matured, or could he simply think his way with characteristic fluency back into the past?

When Wagner updated *Tannhäuser* later in life, and Verdi updated *Macbeth*, each of them had developed to a point in his creativity from which he could no longer have retreated to his previous self. As a result, the new music written for these youthful pieces inevitably sounded like new music, and fitted uneasily into the original context. The newness of Mendelssohn's incidental music – a total of thirteen numbers, vocal and orchestral, commissioned by the King of Prussia for a production in Potsdam – defies such easy identification. Indeed, Mendelssohn would doubtless have been shocked if it had been otherwise. His whole idea was to produce music so attuned to his old style that nobody would notice the difference.

To do so, he took the most meticulous care. His voice, untainted by the passage of time, was as it had always been. The intermezzo is a case in point. A portrait of Hermia's agitation on discovering Lysander's absence, it is written in his most typically refined, elegant yet passionate vein, before swinging captivatingly into comedy for the entrance of Bottom and his mates.

The scherzo, by a lifelong expert in scherzos, is one of the best of its kind – fairy music which is sparkling, mischievous, needle-sharp. The nocturne, depicting the slumbering lovers, is a ravishing study in horn tone. The wedding march, shredded by church organs wherever there is a church organ to shred it, instantly regains its freshness when performed with its proper orchestration and in proper context. Not until Britten's opera on the same subject appeared more than a century later would midsummer magic again be so vividly evoked.

Most recordings of Mendelssohn's *A Midsummer Night's Dream* are edited or abbreviated in some way, but Seiji Ozawa gives us the overture and incidental music complete and in correct order. Since this requires not only the presence of the Boston Symphony Orchestra but also the Tanglewood Festival Chorus, two solo singers (Kathleen Battle and Frederica von Stade) as First and Second Fairies, and the presence, whether you like it or not, of a narrator (Judi Dench), the performance undoubtedly possesses star quality (DG 439 897-2).

Ozawa, as his Edinburgh Festival presentation of Weber's *Oberon* revealed, knows how to handle musical magic. Claudio Abbado's rival recording with the Berlin Philharmonic is disfigured by Kenneth Branagh's irksomely ostentatious narration, far more intrusive than Dench's (Sony SK62826); but André Previn's with the London Symphony Orchestra avoids most of the pitfalls of the score and can be recommended alongside Ozawa (EMI Encore 574981-2).

# Five

## 1827
## STRING QUARTET IN A MINOR, OP. 13

Adagio – Allegro vivace

Adagio non lento

Intermezzo: Allegretto con moto

Presto

Another teenage work of quite extraordinary maturity, Mendelssohn's A minor Quartet, Op. 13, was written in the year of Beethoven's death and pays tribute to that tragedy in at least three significant ways. In the broadest sense, it represents Mendelssohn's emotional response to the great 'late' quartet, Op. 132 in the same key, in which Beethoven thanked God for his (sadly brief) recovery from life-threatening illness. More specifically, it contains in its slow movement a peculiarly poignant, droopingly sinuous fugal section quoting directly from Beethoven's terse F minor Quartet, Op. 95. In addition, it purposefully employs a 'motto' (or recurrent) theme reminiscent of similar motifs which appear and reappear in Beethoven's last quartets.

People eager to find fault with Mendelssohn have pounced on this work as an example of his lack of originality, thereby missing its point entirely. Its Beethovenisms, and the way Mendelssohn uses them, are in fact among its most fascinating features; and motto themes, already exploited by young Schubert, would become a major element in the music of Schumann, Berlioz, Tchaikovsky, Dvořák, Liszt and, above all, Wagner. The vein, indeed, was to continue into the twentieth century, when Shostakovich became obsessed with the recurring musical possibilities of the initials of his own name. In this respect, far from being a backward-looking classicist, Mendelssohn was an innovative composer who, had he lived, might have developed this aspect of his genius far beyond the point he did.

He had already displayed it, in a small but striking way, towards the end of his Octet by bringing back material from the preceding scherzo and infiltrating it into the finale with a grasp of tempo so subtle that the efforts of later composers to do the same can seem crude in comparison. He had also declared in writing that one of his most important musical principles was 'the relation of all four or three or two or one movements of a sonata to each other and their respective parts', a statement which may take a little deciphering but which points again to Mendelssohn's belief in music as an integer.

So here in Op. 13, written at the tender age of 18, the principle was put startlingly into practice – and in a particularly Mendelssohnian way. Though traditionally described as being in A minor, the work begins and ends in the key of A major with a slow motto theme, placed as if within inverted commas and in fact a quotation from one of Mendelssohn's own amorous songs, 'Is es wahr?' (Is it true?), Op. 9, No. 1. The rhythmic resemblance to the recurring motto in the finale of Beethoven's last quartet, Op. 135 in F major – 'Muss es sohn?' (Must it be?) – seems as deliberate as it is unmistakable.

But no less notable, and in this case utterly Mendelssohnian, is the way in which a minor-key work is given such distinctively major-key buttresses. The scheme of major–minor or minor–major was something he would explore again later in other ways, and in the same key of A, when he came to compose his 'Italian' symphony, which is a major-key work with a finale in the minor, and the 'Scotch' symphony, which is a minor-key work with a tailpiece in the major. The tonality of the early quartet, however, remains very special, and very personal. Beethoven, it's true, did something similar in his 'Kreutzer' sonata, a work in A major with minor-key leanings, but lacking the overall unity of the Mendelssohn. The similarity, indeed, is confined to the first movement, in each case a substantial *allegro* in the minor emerging strangely and surprisingly from a slow introduction in the major. In Mendelssohn's finale, however, the process is reversed to greatly satisfying and integrated effect, whereas Beethoven could be said to have lost the plot by incorporating a major-key finale intended for a different work altogether.

Though Mendelssohn's neatly balanced key-scheme, coming as it does from a civilised, enormously gifted teenager, could seem a little too patent, it escapes this accusation through being so profoundly logical. The meaning behind the motto theme in any case remains mysterious and ambiguous. Does it anticipate Schumann in the extra-musical significance of the quoted words ('Is it true?'), with their possible reference to a love affair on which young Mendelssohn had recently embarked, or are the notes themselves all that matter? If so, are they meant to sound as yearning as, in the circumstances, they seem to do? And is the viola trill which leads into the *allegro* merely decorative, or is it something more meaningful than that?

The main body of the first movement invites further speculation, not only because it is so passionately couched in a minor key but also because it contains such a degree of dissonance that Mendelssohn's father, when he heard it, felt prompted to 'rack his brains to discover the composer's thoughts'. Not even when the second of the two main themes arrives on the cello does the music swing into the major, as it might be expected to do. Though the traditional change of key is observed at this point, it is from one minor key into another.

The slow movement in initially warm F major supplies no answers. Even its tempo marking, 'Adagio non lento', seems odd and self-contradictory (essentially 'slow not slow') until we remember that 'adagio' can also mean 'comfortable'. Yet this music, for all its lovely rich melodiousness, has a characteristic Mendelssohnian agitation in its middle section which is seriously at odds with its comfortable aspects, just as the succeeding intermezzo, for all its lightness of touch, is far from being a quicksilver scherzo of the sort which Mendelssohn had already made very much his own.

But intermezzos, like scherzos, were to become a Mendelssohn speciality, later inspiring Brahms to employ the same term for some of the shorter, lighter-weight interior movements of his large-scale works. This one is witty, somewhat whimsical, yet with the same sense of yearning which has intruded earlier in the work.

Then, in the finale, yearning turns to passion, as the dramatic freedom of the introductory recitative fiercely indicates. As in much of Mendelssohn's later chamber music, the first violin plays a leading role, driving the other instruments through passages of restlessness, filled with tense crescendos, diminuendos and a sudden backtrack to the fugal music of the slow movement. After this, the final return to the opening of the first movement sounds absolutely right, the peaceful resolution of a far from peaceful work being beautifully achieved.

Mendelssohn's A minor Quartet needs wholly committed performances. Anything less will simply induce feelings of disappointment, especially if it is played at the end of a concert programme, where it traditionally tends to make people wish they were listening to Beethoven instead. In fact, as a major work with ample intensity of expression and conviction of argument, it should make nobody feel like that. The Coull Quartet's recording, which couples it with Op. 12 (Hyperion CDA 66397), is suitably stirring, as is the Talich Quartet's with the same coupling (Calliope CAL 9311). With performances like these, the music's inspiration is never in doubt.

# Six

## 1829
## STRING QUARTET IN E FLAT MAJOR, OP. 12

Adagio non troppo – Allegro non tardante

Andante espressivo

Canzonetta: Allegretto

Molto allegro e vivace

Mendelssohn's String Quartet in E flat major, Op. 12, was his first quartet to bear an opus number and his first quartet to be published. Yet, coming from a 20-year-old composer whose output was already lavish, it can hardly be called a prentice piece. Upon such niceties of judgement does our perception of Mendelssohn tend to rest, but the matter in this case is complicated by our knowledge that the facts are faulty. This was not actually Mendelssohn's first quartet, nor even his second; and the opus number happens to be wrong.

Though it hardly needs an expert in the art of opus numbers or dates of publication to know that such things are far from foolproof, it is nevertheless surprising that Mendelssohn's Op. 12 was written two years after Op. 13. The music, after all, really does sound as if it preceded that sensationally vanguard masterpiece. But sensationalism apart, Op. 12 was composed at a time of high inspiration by a wealthy, sophisticated, precocious postgraduate who had already declared his genius in several outstanding works. Sailing to Britain soon after his epoch-making resurrection of Bach's *St Matthew Passion* in Berlin in March 1829, he started a grand three-year tour of Europe which inspired some of his most famous works, including the 'Italian' symphony, the 'Scotch' symphony and *The Hebrides* overture.

Among the many people he met, only Sir Walter Scott at Abbotsford greeted him gracelessly and made him feel unwelcome. From everyone else, it seems, he received nothing but kindness; and this 'British' string quartet, which he began to write soon after his arrival in London in the spring and completed just before embarking for Calais in the autumn, is a reflection of his contentment. On reaching France, he noted nostalgically: 'So England lies behind me and my visit is at an end. It is a beautiful and beloved country, and when its white cliffs disappeared and the black French coast came into view, I felt as though I had taken leave of a friend.' It was a friendship he would later seize every opportunity to revive.

Musically, the work confirms Mendelssohn's ability to manipulate the most traditional elements of classical form to achieve a curiously but very satisfyingly unclassical effect. The music critic Paul Driver, putting it another way, has remarked on how, in an even earlier E flat major quartet, Mendelssohn's inspiration was able to burn through craftsmanship and correctitude. Here, however, the burgeoning composer went even further, integrating his material through references to a short recurring motto theme, and employing his youthful admiration for Beethoven (who had died in 1827) to new and creative purpose.

The first movement's resemblance to Beethoven's *Harp* quartet, Op. 74, in the same key and with the same sort of slow introduction, has often been noted, sometimes disparagingly. But though the connection does not seem fortuitous, it simply underlines the fact that the result is not Beethoven but definitely Mendelssohn. The sweet plaintiveness and delicate passion of the melodies, the Mendelssohnian gift of arousing song in the mind of the listener, the first violin's way of leading the action and rising ardently high above the other instruments are very typical characteristics, certainly at this stage in his career. The outcome is a work which quite often sounds more like a violin concerto – more like Mendelssohn's own much later Violin Concerto – than a string quartet.

Mendelssohn's fingerprints are even more visible on the very original minor-key canzonetta, which proceeds unhurriedly, with catlike tread, like a scherzo in slow motion, until it reaches its accelerated middle section, as softly luminous and quicksilverish as anything in *A Midsummer Night's Dream*. No less Mendelssohnian is the slow movement, a heartfelt song without words which grows in intensity until, at the climax, the first violin breaks free from the other instruments with a recitative which Mendelssohn asked to be played 'with fire'.

The slow-moving spell is broken by the intrusion of the urgent and overheated finale, which – in panting dance rhythms anticipating those of the finale of the 'Italian' symphony but quoting material already heard earlier in the quartet – sweeps the music fiercely to its close. Ferocity in Mendelssohn may seem a contradiction in terms, which only goes to show how often he has been, and continues to be, misjudged.

Much of Mendelssohn's chamber music, which forms the emotional heart of his output, remains disgracefully neglected. But happily there are now sufficient recordings of it to convey its range – and the range of ways of performing it. High among these is the Coull Quartet's complete and wonderfully lyrical three-disc set of the seven works along with the four separate quartet movements gathered together as Op. 81, an *intégrale* which fully justifies the financial outlay involved (Hyperion CDS44051/3). Though the Coull's Op. 12 is available separately, coupled conveniently with Op. 13 in A minor and two of the separate quartet movements, it would be an act of parsimony to confine yourself to this single disc (Hyperion CDA66397).

The same two works, minus the short pieces, are available in rival performances by the vivacious, keen-edged young Leipzig Quartet (MDG 307 1055-2), the admirable young British-based Eroica Quartet on period instruments (HM HMU 907245) and the delicately nuanced Quartet

Mosaïques (Auvidis E8622). These and the glorious Czech warmth of the Talich Quartet (Calliope CAL9311), perhaps the best performances of the lot, are enough to suggest, along with a supercharged set from the Emerson Quartet, that a Mendelssohn revival is in the making.

# Seven

## 1832
## SYMPHONY NO. 5 IN D MAJOR, OP. 107 ('REFORMATION')

Andante – Allegro con fuoco　　　Allegro vivace　　　Andante –
Chorale: Ein' feste Burg ist unser Gott – Andante con moto –
Allegro vivace – Allegro maestoso

Dvořák's symphonies took a long time to be correctly numbered, so that the 'New World', established in people's minds as his Fifth Symphony, was eventually hailed as his Ninth. Mendelssohn's symphonies, on the other hand, remain a muddle. If we include the first twelve of them – delightful works for strings which, in the composer's opinion, were too immature to merit publication – in our reckoning, then his 'official' Symphony No. 1 was in fact his thirteenth.

But to number them that way would be no more accurate, because the 'Italian' symphony, traditionally known as No. 4, was composed before the 'Scotch' (No. 3). As for the valedictory 'Reformation' (No. 5), it actually dates from earlier than either of these. What would seem to have been Mendelssohn's last symphony was thus nothing of the sort. As the product of a 21-year-old composer, on the other hand, it was a remarkably mature, self-confident and characteristic work (Haydn and Beethoven at the same age had not produced any symphonies at all). Not only was it coherent and purposeful in structure, but also, like the succeeding 'Hymn of Praise', it forged its own special Mendelssohnian link between church and concert hall.

In the case of the 'Reformation' symphony, moreover, Mendelssohn achieved this without requiring the help of a chorus. Its religious references – the chorale-like orchestration of Martin Luther's setting of Psalm 46, *Ein' feste Burg* ('A Safe Stronghold'), and its quoting of Johann Naumann's *Dresden Amen* half a century before Wagner employed it in *Parsifal* – were all conceived in symphonic terms with a combination of brilliance and solemnity entirely suited to the occasion that was the symphony's *raison d'être*. Indeed, the tercentenary of the Augsburg Protestant Confession of 1530, through which the Lutheran Church displaced Catholicism in Germany, could not have found a composer better equipped or more appropriate than Mendelssohn to celebrate it.

Young though he was at the time, Mendelssohn's grasp of what was needed – the creative use of *Ein' feste Burg* as the climax of the symphonic argument and what now seems the uncanny foretaste of Wagner in the stealthy appearances of the *Dresden Amen* in the first movement – was audaciously assured. Yet the work never had the auspicious send-off it deserved. The 1830 premiere was postponed. A performance in Paris two years later was cancelled because the players deemed the music too didactic. Not until Mendelssohn made revisions was it finally unveiled in Berlin in November 1832, with the composer himself as conductor. Even today, it falls far short of the 'Italian' and 'Scotch' symphonies in popularity. But this at least has the advantage of making every performance of it seem like a revelation.

In addition to its religious back-references, the work also contains a symphonic one, declaimed in the slow introduction to the first movement in conjunction with the *Dresden Amen*. So clearly do we hear the opening fanfare of Haydn's 'London' symphony at this point that the resemblance hardly seems coincidental – but then, as Mendelssohn must have been equally aware, the notes also have a kinship with *Ein' feste Burg*. The main *allegro* section of the movement is in his stormiest vein, with swirling anticipations of the *Hebrides* overture, but the poetic highpoint is the softly inspired reappearance of the *Dresden Amen* just before the subdued start of the recapitulation.

The two central movements are more in the manner of intermezzi, the first of them a fleet and gracefully swaying Mendelssohn scherzo, charmingly orchestrated, the second a rather operatic song – or recitative – without words, from a composer with no great flair for opera. Yet the fact that he was contemplating an opera at the time of his death is one more symbol of a composer permanently short of time.

This movement – no more than an extended linking passage – serves as an introduction to the finale, which is announced with a gradually swelling delivery of *Ein' feste Burg* (another theme Wagner would subsequently employ, this time in his *Kaisermarsch*). It is towards this sonorous chorale that the earlier portion of the work has clearly been heading – indeed, one Mendelssohn authority has gone so far as to describe the first three movements as 'preludes'. From then on, the music is driven symphonically to its destination with appropriate grandeur and exuberance, shot through with occasional moments of delectable Mendelssohnian sweetness.

Record companies have never shown much interest in Mendelssohn's 'Reformation' symphony, though Sir Thomas Beecham, who adored this composer, persuaded EMI to let him record it on three-and-a-half 78rpm shellac discs soon after the Second World War. But his efforts to rehabilitate this splendid work fell on stony ground, and since then there has been nobody with the right mixture of élan and elegance to convey the full inspiration of the music.

Beecham's ability to turn a phrase like nobody else is confirmed by John Eliot Gardiner's more prosaic performance with the Vienna Philharmonic. In all other respects, however, and thanks particularly to the sound of the Viennese brass, this is the modern recording to go for. The coupling, which places the established version of the 'Italian' symphony alongside

Mendelssohn's startlingly detailed and almost unknown revision of it, makes this disc an irresistible choice (DGG 459 156-2).

Claudio Abbado's spirited performance with the London Symphony Orchestra forms part of his four-disc bargain-price box containing all five of the symphonies and three of the overtures (DG 471 467-2). This is a safe recommendation, as is the Bernard Haitink recording which, with the Concertgebouw Orchestra and London Philharmonic, crams the 'Reformation' and 'Italian' symphonies, the *Midsummer Night's Dream* music, the *Calm Sea and Prosperous Voyage* overture and the Violin Concerto, with the great Arthur Grumiaux as soloist, very desirably on to two half-price discs (Philips Duo 456 074-2).

Nor is Lorin Maazel's recording of the 'Reformation' to be sniffed at, even with Cesar Franck's Symphony in D minor as coupling. Here, the Berlin Philharmonic's brass players compete with Vienna's, giving Mendelssohn's symphony just the impact it deserves (DG 449 720-2).

# Eight

## 1832
## OVERTURE, *THE HEBRIDES*, OP. 26

Great composers who visited Britain in the nineteenth century seldom ventured as far north as Scotland. Berlioz was prevented from doing so in 1853, when the Glasgow Choral Union turned down his offer to conduct Mendelssohn's *Elijah*. Mendelssohn himself did rather better in 1829, even if, between the Tweed and the Hebrides, he encountered a famously unfriendly Sir Walter Scott at Abbotsford. Scott, it seems, was on the point of going out when Mendelssohn arrived, and was no more receptive to the composer's letter of introduction than was Goethe by the fifty songs sent to him on behalf of a mediocrity called Franz Schubert. As Mendelssohn put it with appropriate petulance, he 'drove eighty miles and lost a day for the sake of at best one half-hour of superficial conversation'.

But Holyrood Palace, at least, inspired the opening of his 'Scotch' symphony (as well as, rather curiously, that of his supernatural *Die erste Walpurgisnacht*). The scenery of Dunkeld and Blair Atholl made the prospect of crossing the mountains on foot to Inveraray seem inviting. And his voyage to Fingal's Cave on the island of Staffa prompted his *Hebrides* overture. In a letter home, he wrote of how 'extraordinarily' the seascapes had affected him – they certainly made him extraordinarily seasick – and he enclosed twenty-one bars of music that had sprung to mind there. These formed the start of his *Hebrides* overture, though the work was not completed until he reached Italy the following year. It was then, as one of his biographers later commented, 'among the laurels and orange groves that his thoughts and affections carried him back to the waves of the North Sea and the oak-forests of Germany'.

Though he was undecided about the work's title – *The Solitary Island*, *The Isles of Fingal* and (particularly favoured) *Fingal's Cave* were among the possibilities – the music itself was gradually materialising. Most of it grows from the flowing, repeated phrase with which it opens. Wagner, who appreciated it more than he admitted, called it an 'aquarelle', and compared one passage – the source perhaps of his own *Flying Dutchman* overture – to the wailing of sea winds.

Yet, for the most part, Mendelssohn's is a seascape recollected in tranquillity, an atmospheric tone poem rather than an overture, and the most evocative picture of northern waters before Sibelius's *The Oceanides*. Not even the rough waves that rise towards the end (where the pace quickens, the strings surge, and trumpets and drums inject an element of danger into the music) are allowed to disrupt the formal perfection of the score.

When the storm subsides, we can expect the little introductory motif to return, and so it does. Earlier in the overture, it even inspires the theme of the second subject, first heard on bassoons and cellos and ultimately, in a poetically extended form, on the clarinets. Edinburgh's distinguished musical essayist, Donald Francis Tovey, declared this to be quite the greatest melody Mendelssohn ever wrote. Among its virtues, however, is the fact that it is never overstated or repeated once too often – though it does require a conductor who can contrast it sufficiently with the opening theme.

Even on its first appearance, this second theme makes its point without disturbing the natural flow of the music. Is it therefore just one more example of Mendelssohnian facility? Or is it something more subtle than that? Subtlety, surely, is the answer. Though there may be works by Mendelssohn that tread a tightrope between the one and the other, the grey and silver beauty of the *Hebrides* overture – perhaps the most perfect of all musical seascapes – shows the hand of a master.

It was not, of course, Mendelssohn's only overture. Though opera was never his métier, he found varied and excellent reasons for writing overtures which did not need to have operas attached to them. One which could have done, and should have done, was *A Midsummer Night's Dream*, written with the utmost flair at the age of 17. The subsequent incidental music, commissioned for a production of Shakespeare's comedy, showed what was possible. Similarly tantalising was the *Ruy Blas* overture of 1839. Composed for a play (by Victor Hugo) which Mendelssohn loathed, it was surely the best and most dramatic overture of its period, brazenly bridging the gap between Weber and Wagner.

In contrast, *Calm Sea and Prosperous Voyage* (really a pair of tableaux, like Beethoven's Goethe-inspired cantata of the same title) and *The Beautiful Melusine* were fine watercolours in the manner of *The Hebrides*, but between them they constitute a group of works which form a special section of Mendelssohn's output. Buying them as a bunch, rather than as fillers for recordings of other works, would make sense, if conductors and record companies could be persuaded to see the point. Claus Peter Flor seems to have needed no persuasion, if his recording of most of these (plus two other) overtures with the admirable Bamberg Symphony Orchestra is anything to go by (RCA 2CD 74321 84600-2).

What is needed now, however, is a recording of the accurate new edition of *The Hebrides*, which differs in fine detail from the standard version and, for that reason, has the power to deliver small but startling frissons. Even without that asset, however, the Scottish Chamber Orchestra's performance differs from others through its employment of properly scaled forces, greatly to the advantage of the music's texture and, in particular, the translucent woodwind parts which other performances obscure. Recorded in Edinburgh in 2002, this disc, by including the

Violin Concerto and the 'Scotch' symphony, adds up to a very satisfactory Mendelssohn concert, with Joseph Swensen, the orchestra's principal conductor, not only directing the performances but also proving himself a vivacious soloist (Linn CKD 205).

# Nine

## 1832
## *DIE ERSTE WALPURGISNACHT*, OP. 60

Ballade for soloists, chorus and orchestra

*Elijah*, whether we like it or not, has to be Mendelssohn's choral masterpiece; but its pagan obverse, *Die erste Walpurgisnacht* ('The First Walpurgis Night'), is really much more fun. Why, then, does it remain so neglected? Partly, no doubt, because nobody believes Mendelssohn could have made a success of a subject so sacrilegious, and few conductors feel disposed to find out. Mendelssohn, of all composers, roistering with witches? Mendelssohn, who complained that he needed a wash after fingering one of Berlioz's scores? Forget it!

Think of *Die erste Walpurgisnacht* as another *Midsummer Night's Dream*, however, and his interest in it begins to make sense. The words of Goethe's ballade were a further attraction. Originally, they were to have been set by Mendelssohn's teacher, Carl Zelter, who received them from the illustrious poet in person. Failing to be inspired by them, Zelter passed them on to Mendelssohn, who took them with him to Vienna and then to Italy, contemplating them amid the ruins and landscapes of the south.

Having been compared by Goethe to the 'divine' Mozart, Mendelssohn was prepared to accept the challenge. He had just written *The Hebrides* overture and was feeling his way into the 'Italian' and 'Scotch' symphonies. For better or worse, musical scene-painting was on his mind; and the overture to *Die erste Walpurgisnacht* opens with the same dourly descriptive theme, entitled 'Bad Weather', which also starts the 'Scotch' symphony.

Mendelssohn was strong on concert overtures, and this one, for all its unfamiliarity, is among his best – a vivid progress through menacing winter storm clouds into the soft sunshine of spring, Walpurgis Night being a celebration of the coming of May. But when the chorus, impersonating Druids, start to sing of sacrificial fires, and learn what will befall them if they are trapped by the Christians, the music shifts ground. Is this an opera that we see before us? No, it is a secular cantata, but on its own idiosyncratic terms it possesses real dramatic thrust.

It is also – which makes it unique in Mendelssohn's output – a satire on religious superstition. Its supernatural elements need to be taken with a pinch of salt; and its central anthem, 'Come with Prongs and Pitchforks', is in fact an anti-anthem, the only one of its kind Mendelssohn wrote. Beginning as a soft nocturnal march, it gains in grotesquerie ('let owl and hoopoe screech amid our roundelay') and ends with the Christians being scattered by the magic of the Druid priest. The music, in keeping with Goethe's text, has humour as well as drama.

Lasting upwards of half an hour, the ballade shows Mendelssohn using his skills with a fake seriousness which never becomes trivial. There is an almost Gilbert-and-Sullivan-like element – and England's great musical partnership, we should remember, adored Mendelssohn – about the effect of warriors creeping through a wood to the strains of an elfin Mendelssohn scherzo. As for the closing Hymn to Faith, it anticipates *Elijah* while at the same time mocking the whole idea of such an oratorio.

Berlioz, whose music Mendelssohn so despised, naturally saw the point of *Die erste Walpurgisnacht* and called it a masterpiece of romanticism. Two excellent recordings of it show him to have been right. Nikolaus Harnoncourt's live performance in Graz's Stefaniensaal has multiple benefits: a wonderful lightness of touch, the gleaming sound of the Chamber Orchestra of Europe, the presence of the superb Arnold Schoenberg Choir, and Harnoncourt's obvious belief in what he is doing.

The coupling, a generous, well-chosen selection of movements from *A Midsummer Night's Dream*, stresses the connections between the two works and places the *Walpurgisnacht* in its logical context. Though the spoken narration and the vocal music, with Pamela Coburn a bright soprano soloist, are performed in German, it all underlines that Mendelssohn's is nothing if not a German *Dream*. An English translation is included (Teldec 9031-74882-2).

Alternatively, there is Claus Peter Flor, one of the younger generation of German conductors, whose recording with the Bamberg Symphony Chorus and Orchestra (supposedly an outfit of the second rank but often capable of outclassing its superiors) is no less piquant, and alert to every detail of the music. The coupling, a group of Mendelssohn songs with and without words, employs perceptive orchestral arrangements by Siegfried Matthus, with Deon van der Walt as soloist. Though hardly as essential as *A Midsummer Night's Dream*, it's a nice way to fill out a bewitching disc (RCA 09026 62513-2).

A rare performance by Joseph Swensen and the Scottish Chamber Orchestra and Choir in Edinburgh in 2002, with the performers spilling off the platform all over the main body of the Queen's Hall, was exhilarating enough to have deserved a commemoration recording. A pity it never happened.

As for *Elijah*, if you really feel your Mendelssohn collection would be incomplete without the religious experience which the Victorian critic Henry Chorley hailed as 'not only the sacred work of our time' but a work 'for our children and our children's children', then the Israel Philharmonic and Leipzig Radio Chorus form an ideal partnership under Kurt Masur's refreshingly fast-paced direction, with Alistair Miles suitably sonorous in the title role (Teldec 9031-73131-2).

Scottish buyers, however, may understandably prefer Paul Daniel's scarcely less vivid though more rigidly conducted version with the

Edinburgh Festival Chorus and Orchestra of the Age of Enlightenment, not least because Elijah is impersonated by Bryn Terfel in tones of true Old Testament thunder (Decca 455 688-2DH2). Choice, in the end, may boil down to whether you want it sung in powerful German (Masur) or in the words of the English Bible, as at its Birmingham premiere in 1846 (Daniel).

*Mendelssohn, though he was an able violinist and viola player, was above all a famed virtuoso pianist who could play with charm and fire. His works for piano were an important part of his output, yet tend today to be brushed aside by pianists intent on performing Bach, Beethoven, Schubert and Schumann. Our knowledge of Mendelssohn, however, would be seriously incomplete if we, too, took this severe attitude to his piano music. Though much of it is too difficult for domestic performance, enough of it has been recorded to give an impression of what we are missing.*

# Ten

## 1833
## PHANTASIE IN F SHARP MINOR, OP. 28
## ('SONATE ECOSSAISE')

Con moto agitato          Allegro con moto          Presto

The experienced listener knows to be wary of works entitled 'Scottish Fantasy'. Max Bruch's showpiece for violin and orchestra, with 'Scots wha hae' as its climax, is a case in point. But Mendelssohn's Scottish 'fantasy sonata' for solo piano is not like that at all. For a start, it does not sound Scottish, though it is a product of the same tour of Scotland which yielded the *Hebrides* overture and the 'Scotch' symphony. Secondly, it is written in the promising key of F sharp minor, which in Mendelssohn's day tended to denote serious intentions, with remnants of eighteenth-century storm and stress. In addition, its inspiration not only lies in Mendelssohn's own instrument, the piano, but also is of a quality quite as high as that of the more familiar *Variations Sérieuses*, the magnificent post-Bachian, pre-Busonian Fugue in F minor, and the glorious array of *Songs withoutWords*.

Its continued neglect, therefore, is mysterious, though that is a fate which more than one Mendelssohn masterpiece has suffered. In fact, as a model of Mendelssohn style, it could hardly be bettered. Like almost all his most characteristic works, it is simultaneously forward-looking and rooted in classical procedures. His beloved Bach was clearly its fountainhead, as the introductory baroque figuration confirms. Its title, along with the structure and choice of key, suggests a possible link with Beethoven's 'Moonlight' sonata in C sharp minor, which, it should be remembered, was subtitled 'quasi una fantasia', or 'almost' a fantasy. But it has connections also with Schumann's great C major Fantasy, Op. 17, which, appearing three years later, marked a further stage in the history of this sort of work.

Not the least interesting of its features, however, remains its Beethovenian element. Mendelssohn's debt to his powerful predecessor, here and elsewhere, was no conventional piece of purloining. Steeped as a teenager in Beethoven's last works, he was obviously influenced by their idiosyncratic musical language and terse use of counterpoint, yet took pains not simply to copy it. As Charles Rosen has pointed out in his book, *The Romantic Generation*, what was impressive about Mendelssohn's youthful imitations was their outrageous ambition and the nature of their success. 'Far from being a second-hand reproduction of Beethoven's ideas,' he asserted, 'they are individual and personal – in short, peculiarly Mendelssohnian.'

In fact, Mendelssohn was a composer who Mendelssohnised everything he touched, in a manner which could seem almost prophetic of Stravinsky. Sometimes in his responses to Beethoven he did not succeed, but when he did the result was an uncanny assumption of the other composer's identity. As Rosen has put it, 'Mendelssohn recognised himself in Beethoven'.

On the other hand, it is not always so easy to recognise Beethoven in Mendelssohn. The whole point of the Phantasie in F sharp minor is that it is not the 'Moonlight' sonata, even if the first movement is a rippling tone painting, the second is a scherzo and the finale is an agitated *presto* comparable with Beethoven's concluding *presto agitato*. If, in a wholly Mendelssohnian way, this finale sounds even more scherzo-like than the preceding movement, the effect is by no means lopsided. Its sonata-form structure befits its position in the overall scheme of the work, and the music becomes a cumulative, though never superficial, exercise in keyboard velocity.

Performances of Mendelssohn's Phantasie are sadly but predictably rare, and recordings are similarly few. 'Great' pianists, for reasons of their own, tend to sidestep the work, perhaps considering it to be more trouble than it is worth. Pianists who really care about the piece tend to be less career-conscious – artists, in other words, of the second rank, to whom the music matters more than their own egos. When the player is as perceptive as Benjamin Frith, we should rejoice that this is so. His bargain-price recording is just what the music needs, and forms part of an entire Mendelssohn recital which includes the Capriccio, Op. 5, and some vivid tributes to Bach (Naxos 8.553541).

The key to the *Variations Sérieuses*, another work which receives far less than its due, is held by Alfred Brendel, whose recording places it in the context of sets of variations by Mozart, Brahms and Liszt – an admirable idea in which each of the composers perfectly counterbalances the others in keenly gleaming performances (Philips 426 272-2). The domesticity of the *Songs without Words*, the first of which was a touching little gift to his sister Fanny, is caught by Livia Rev in beautifully characterised performances (Hyperion Dyad CDD 22020).

These rival the long-established, resourcefully performed but less intimate set by Daniel Barenboim (DG Double ADD 453 061-2, two discs for the price of one). Listeners are warned, however, that the *Songs without Words* were not intended for long-sustained listening. Heard in bulk, they dwindle to the level of background music in a way in which Schumann's sets of short pieces never do. But, heard by the handful, they succinctly make their poetic point and reveal Mendelssohn's keen mastery of ever-changing moods.

In comparison, the E minor Fugue, composed in 1827 though not published until ten years later, is in his grandest vein. Charles Rosen has hailed the opening as 'the most superb pastiche of Bach ever produced with nineteenth-century means', which may seem a bit like faint praise but is clearly not intended as such.

Nor, when he remarks that Mendelssohn was the inventor of religious kitsch in music, is he mocking Bach's nineteenth-century successor. What Mendelssohn gives us in his E minor Fugue is not only his own vein of Bachian counterpoint but his own approach to what baroque practice is about in purely church terms. One of its cadences, claims Rosen, evokes 'in beautifully worked out detail' the quiet folding of hands in prayer. 'It is obvious', he adds, 'that in the early nineteenth century a reverent whisper was the proper tone to adopt in church.' Mendelssohn's concert fugue, therefore, is not only a fugue but also a character piece.

More than that, it is 'intended as a practical work for a virtuoso to take on tour'. Rosen, as a touring virtuoso, presumably does so; but few others seize this advantage, it must be said. As a result, they lose the chance to champion a work which moves from an 'ostentatiously humble opening' through a continuous acceleration of tempo until it reaches a 'furious allegro' and a 'romantic display of octaves for the left hand alone', reflecting Bach's cadenzas for pedal keyboard in some of the great organ toccatas and fugues. As Rosen sums up: 'Virtuosity, for Bach, was not out of place in a church; for Mendelssohn, religion was not out of place in the concert hall'.

The E minor Fugue, in another words, is a magnificent work, disgracefully neglected today. To sample it for yourself, Benjamin Frith's recording, on the same disc as the Phantasie, is the one to turn to (Naxos 8.553541).

# Eleven

## 1833
## SYMPHONY NO. 4 IN A MAJOR, OP. 90 ('ITALIAN')

Allegro vivace

Con moto moderato

Andante con moto

Saltarello: Presto

The prim young Mendelssohn had no time for the audacious Berlioz's music, dismissing the counterpoint as 'barbarous' and the orchestration as 'so messy and slapdash that you want to wash your hands after going through one of his works'. Berlioz, on the other hand, had plenty of time for Mendelssohn, admiring the finesse of *Fingal's Cave* and conducting the 'Italian' symphony with such mastery in London that the music critic of *The Times* declared that every tempo had been gauged to perfection for the first time in his experience. Both composers, as it happened, were superb conductors, and on one occasion exchanged batons as tokens of mutual esteem, Berlioz admitting that his 'heavy oak cudgel' hardly bore comparison with Mendelssohn's 'sceptre'.

Yet Berlioz's admiration for Mendelssohn's 'Italian' symphony went beyond his ability to conduct it, special though that was. The music – or at any rate its inspiration – dated from the Italian period in both their lives, when Mendelssohn, at the age of 21, was on his second grand tour of Europe, and Berlioz, at 28, had won the Prix de Rome which resulted in his truculent sojourn in the Eternal City.

Mendelssohn, more open-minded in his response and much encouraged by his idol Goethe's experiences as a distinguished traveller in Italy, savoured the 'supreme delight in life' displayed by the Italians. Venice was predictably his first stop. To Naples he took 'three shirts and Goethe's poems'. But Rome, which Berlioz so despised, was the real revelation. In all its ancient columns, he declared, music lay hidden. Not even when he encountered Berlioz – disgruntled as ever with the atmosphere of the 'odious' Caffé Greco (today packed with Japanese tourists and their designer shopping bags) near the Spanish Steps – was his enthusiasm dampened.

Vowing to write an Italian symphony in tribute to the vivacity of the people, he promised that it would be the 'jolliest' piece he had ever produced. Soon he was writing home to say he was making progress. Yet, as with Berlioz and his 'Harold in Italy' symphony of the same period, he stressed that 'symphony' was the word that mattered, rather than any descriptive title. Otherwise, or so he suspected, listeners might mistake his efforts for just another piece of nineteenth-century musical landscape painting, which was far from his intention. It was the sort of topic the two composers discussed while out riding together in the Roman Campagna.

Be that as it may, the Italian features of Mendelssohn's Symphony No. 4 are unmistakable and remain part of its charm, just as the Italian side of 'Harold in Italy' (Berlioz's Symphony No. 2) is one of its poetic pleasures. Both works are symphonies of genius and originality, but it would be puritanical to deny them their picturesque aspects. By the time of the 'Italian' symphony's first performance, which Mendelssohn himself conducted in London in 1833, the symphonic and visual aspects of the music had wholly gelled, just as they were to do in Berlioz's masterpiece, completed the following year. The similarity between their slow movements – Mendelssohn's a sort of pilgrims' march, Berlioz's actually entitled *Pilgrims' March* – is not their only shared feature, though it is certainly the most striking one.

But while the four movements of Berlioz's symphony are unquestionably Byronic in mood, those of Mendelssohn's are less specific. Though Schumann's belief that the 'Scotch' symphony was really the 'Italian', and vice versa, today hardly cuts much ice, there does seem little doubt that the slow movement of the 'Italian' actually has nothing to do with Italy but was intended to commemorate Goethe and Zelter (Mendelssohn's teacher, whose Goethe-inspired *König in Thule* it quotes), both of whom had died in 1832. What the 'Scotch' and 'Italian' symphonies do quite curiously have in common are aspects of the key of A, the 'Scotch' beginning in A minor and ending in A major, the 'Italian' beginning in A major and ending in A minor. In this respect, the one work could be called the obverse of the other, though to what extent this was intentional is impossible to say.

What is easier to identify is the glowing sunniness of the first movement of the 'Italian' – something in no sense Scottish – and the Mediterranean swirl of the finale, which Mendelssohn took pains to entitle *Saltarello*, in tribute to the leaping Italian dance relentlessly evoked by the music. In comparison, the slow movement heads in a different direction, its inspiration surely being the *allegretto* of Beethoven's Seventh Symphony, another study in the relationship between A minor and A major. As for the elfin grace of the third movement – a Mendelssohnian evocation of a classical minuet – its poetic trio section, filled with magical horn calls, could easily have come straight out of *A Midsummer Night's Dream*.

Yet, for all its perfection, the 'Italian' symphony as we know it is in reality no more than an interim report on Mendelssohn's Italian experiences. Surprisingly dissatisfied with many aspects of the work, he embarked in 1834 on a substantial revision of three of its four movements, changing the colouring of the *andante*, adding fresh touches of poetry to the third movement, and considerably extending the finale.

Whatever plans he had for the opening movement were never realised. But his revision of the rest of the work remained unperformed for a century and a half – is authentic Mendelssohn less desirable than authentic Mozart or Beethoven? – and has only now been issued in a performing version upon which most conductors are turning deaf ears. Though it is unlikely by now to replace the original, it sheds fascinating new light on the music.

This is the version characteristically employed by John Eliot Gardiner, side by side with the one we all know, in his recording with the Vienna Philharmonic. A stirring account of the 'Reformation' symphony serves as makeweight (DG 459 156-2). Claudio Abbado's coupling of the 'Italian' and 'Scotch' symphonies with the London Symphony Orchestra offers more conventional pleasures (DG 427 810-2), and Roger Norrington's with the London Classical Players has a translucent lightness of touch which is very refreshing (Virgin 5 61735-2).

# Twelve

## 1833
## OVERTURE, *THE BEAUTIFUL MELUSINE*,
## OP. 32

Mendelssohn thought his *Melusine* overture 'the best' and 'most intimate' thing he had ever produced, an opinion shared, as he informed his sister Fanny in a letter, by many of the people who heard him conduct it in Leipzig in 1836. On the other hand, as he admitted, he was irked by what he considered to be an excessively descriptive review it received in the influential *Musikalische Zeitung*. 'The rigmarole about red coral and green sea-beasts and magic castles and deep seas is all rubbish and astonishes me', he expostulated. Perhaps the critic confused it with *The Hebrides*, which had already been performed and was destined to be a more popular work.

But *Melusine* is nevertheless a lovely piece, sufficiently watery in its imagery to incorporate an unmistakable foretaste of the rippling prelude to *Das Rheingold*, in which the notoriously anti-semitic Wagner paid direct tribute to a composer he professed to deplore. While writing it, Mendelssohn was in fact a resident of the Rhineland, working as musical director in Düsseldorf, conducting at the Lower Rhine Festival, developing his talents as a Sunday landscape painter and, on one occasion, bathing naked in the river when the Queen of Bavaria's boat sailed round a bend. As the supposedly prim composer remarked later, 'We dived *a tempo* into the water just as she approached'. Well, at least it was not Queen Victoria.

The inspiration of the overture lay obliquely in an opera by Conradin Kreutzer (1780–1849) which the suave but irritable Mendelssohn had heard and disliked. Annoyed by the fact that, at the performance he attended, Kreutzer's overture was encored, he reported that he would like to write a better one, which people 'wouldn't encore but would receive more inwardly'. With his love for musical gossamer, the story of The Beautiful Melusine, a myth about a water sprite, suited him to perfection. His mellifluous opening theme immediately catches the mood, and the other themes sustain it. Yet there is more than mellowness here. As Edinburgh's distinguished musical essayist, Donald Francis Tovey, once pointed out, the overture has an underlying agitation and sorrow, in no way diminished by the fact that the context is that of a fairy tale.

Mendelssohn and Kreutzer were not the only composers whose attention was drawn to the melancholy tale of the water sprite who was permitted to marry a mortal on condition that her true nature was concealed. Beethoven had been offered the Grillparzer libretto ahead of Kreutzer but was too busy with his Ninth Symphony to do anything about it. For posterity, this was a stroke of luck. A Beethoven *Melusine* does not sound like one of musical history's great missed opportunities.

Dvořák's *Rusalka*, on the other hand, is a successful variation on the same theme, full of Freudian undercurrents fascinatingly explored by David Pountney's (waterless) production for English National Opera. Aribert Reimann's *Melusine*, an operatic update with a similarly landlocked heroine, had its British premiere at the 1971 Edinburgh Festival but failed to achieve lift-off. Tchaikovsky's *Swan Lake* and Henze's *Ondine* tell similar tales in the form of ballets.

All of them, from Grillparzer onwards, share a degree of symbolism unlikely to be lost on students of modern psychoanalysis. Grillparzer's Melusine, inspiration of Mendelssohn's overture, marries Count Raymond of Lusignan in the hope that he will never discover she is a fish from the waist down. But, having sworn to let her leave him once a month at the time of the full moon, he breaks his oath by following her to the lake which is her secret habitat and discovering what she really is. His fate is to lose her forever; but, rather than suffer this, he throws himself into the water and drowns in her arms.

Though the art of the concert overture had its principal source in Beethoven, Mendelssohn developed it into something wholly different with *The Hebrides* and *Melusine*, in which poetic and pictorial elements gained a new importance. In France, Berlioz was doing the same in his *Corsaire* and *King Lear* overtures – his *Waverley* overture indeed predated *The Hebrides* – and later composers would see the wisdom of identifying such works more precisely as 'tone poems' or 'symphonic poems'.

Certainly, *Melusine* was symphonic enough to be written in sonata form, even if the poetic characterisation of the music rather conceals the fact. Thus there are themes suggestive of Melusine's mysterious beauty and of the Count's suspicions which, at the same time, carry structural significance. There is despairing music which, at the same time, forms some sort of 'development' section. And there is a calm ending which seems as much about Mendelssohn as about Melusine.

The entire work, indeed, is an exquisitely crafted example of Mendelssohnian understatement which falls to pieces if the conductor, as some conductors do, hammers it into the ground. Claudio Abbado, committed to Mendelssohn though he is, has been guilty of this bludgeoning approach to a work whose passion is all the better for being discreet. His recording of it, however, need not impede enjoyment of the generously priced Mendelssohn box of which it forms part (DG 471 467-2, four discs).

The most truthful performance, in which the waters lap lightly and the themes are shaped with the utmost elegance, remains the one which Sir Thomas Beecham conducted soon after his founding of the Royal Philharmonic Orchestra. Though the recording is rough – the performance originally required two black 78rpm shellac discs – the tone quality shines through, and the two-disc CD set is a marvellous array of Beecham lollipops ranging from Dvořák's *Golden Spinning Wheel* to Saint-Saëns's *Rouet d'Omphale* (Dutton Laboratories 2CDEA 5026).

# Thirteen

## 1838
## SONATA FOR VIOLIN AND PIANO IN F MAJOR

Allegro vivace                    Adagio                    Assai vivace

Mendelssohn's two cello sonatas are masterly contributions to a repertoire less packed with riches than it should be. Two of his three violin sonatas, on the other hand, are masterpieces which, within a very crowded repertoire, have simply never been given their due. Why this should be is hard to say, though easy enough to guess. The earlier of the two, Op. 4 in F minor, has been widely scorned by Mendelssohn authorities, not least Philip Radcliffe, the composer's distinguished but depressingly negative *Master Musicians* biographer, who disgracefully dismissed it as being 'on the whole the weakest and most colourless of all Mendelssohn's chamber works'. All he really meant, of course, was that he didn't like it.

The other and later work, in F major, may have been deprived of the official stamp of an opus number, but that does not mean it lacks the stamp of genius, even if Mendelssohn himself seemed to care little for it. It is simply one of those works – his dozen or so precocious symphonies for strings and the early D minor Violin Concerto (not to be confused with the great E minor) are others – which were allowed to gather dust and which, as a result, remain underplayed and unappreciated.

Yet the sheer verve of the F major Sonata – discovered, edited, published and championed by Yehudi Menuhin, to whom we are also indebted for the rediscovery of the D minor Violin Concerto – singles it out as something special. Perhaps its multiplicity of notes, and the strain it thereby places on performers, form a challenge which some recitalists are unwilling to face. But it is a fascinating work in whose slow movement the brilliant young Mendelssohn can be heard maturing into someone emotionally more complex.

Though only 29 when he wrote it, Mendelssohn (like Schubert before him) was by then already an immensely productive and experienced composer. But the claim that he had already passed his peak was an assumption the F major Sonata easily disproves. The first movement, which gives the impression of being in mid-flight before it even begins, has the exhilarating agility of the E minor Violin Concerto, which he composed soon afterwards. Here, indeed, is the very essence of the composer, unleashed with a velocity which the great string Octet had long ago shown him to be capable of, and which the concerto would rekindle. If there are moments when Beethoven stalks through this movement, it is Beethoven in his Mendelssohn guise, and all the more captivating as a result.

The passion of the *adagio* – emerging from a composer more famed for fluency than for fire – shows him searching for, and finding, a new musical language. The finale, in contrast, is a *moto perpetuo* of almost Paganini-like bravura. Why Mendelssohn felt this work to be unworthy of publication remains a mystery. But then, it should be remembered, he felt much the same about his 'Italian' symphony, of which he wrote two versions, neither of which satisfied him.

It is hardly surprising, therefore, that there are very few recordings of Mendelssohn's F major and F minor sonatas, though one particular coupling is so good, and throws such sympathetic light upon them, that the performances can only be hailed as irresistible. Shlomo Mintz, the Russian-born Israeli, is the violinist, Paul Ostrovsky the pianist; with a united sweetness of tone and exhilarating agility, they bring each work into exact Mendelssohnian focus, missing nothing in terms of poignancy and radiance of expression. This is Mendelssohn playing par excellence, as responsive to the mature F major work as to the juvenile F minor (DG 474 690-2).

Felix Ayo's recording of the same two works has the advantage of including a further sonata, his very first, confusingly also in F major, composed at the age of 11. Even if not quite in the class of the others, it is not something you would dismiss as a piece of juvenilia. Mendelssohn did not write that sort of music. Though the veteran director of I Musici plays less sweetly than Mintz, these are nevertheless finely articulated performances, with the expert Bruno Canino as pianist (Dynamic CDS 180).

# Fourteen

## 1838
## STRING QUARTET IN E FLAT MAJOR, OP. 44, NO. 3

Allegro vivace

Adagio non troppo

Scherzo: Assai leggiero

Molto allegro con fuoco

Felix Mendelssohn, it could be said, was the Leonard Bernstein of his day. Composer, conductor, pianist, poet, painter, prodigy, writer, athlete, linguist, lecturer, traveller, he mastered everything he touched. But his works surpassed with ease those of his modern American counterpart, and he died much younger, at a time when – as later generations decreed – his inspiration was already in serious decline.

For evidence to the contrary, the neglected F minor string quartet, Op. 80, composed just after his sister's death and just before his own, is worth hearing. Music so passionate in its desolation, so private in its anguish, was hardly the product of a *wunderkind* who had suffered early burnout. But then, none of Mendelssohn's quartets – eight of them in all, if you include the unnumbered quartet from his teenage years and the composite quartet published posthumously – has really been given its due.

The E flat major, Op. 44, No. 3 – the third of his quartets to be written in a key whose warmth of tone he clearly found inspiring – is a case in point. Conspicuously the longest of all his quartets, it magnificently confirms Mendelssohn's special ability, from very early in his career, to employ the most traditional elements of classical form in a way which was not really classical at all. It is a trait also to be found in Berlioz's music, which Mendelssohn affected to despise, though the two men had more in common than either of them believed.

The resultant work, at any rate, contains not a drop of the enervating blandness of which Mendelssohn, even at his best, has been too often accused. To claim that its energy is of a sort which had already reached its apogee in the great string Octet, composed at the age of 16, is to fall into the trap which has led to the undervaluing of so many of his later works – and Mendelssohn's later works, we should remember, were almost as 'early' as Schubert's or, indeed, Purcell's. What the music by then was undeniably beginning to lose, in spite of its vivacity, was some of its youthful playfulness. But what it was gaining was a fresh freedom of utterance in which exuberance could turn to something close to violence and in which even the elfin lightness of a Mendelssohn scherzo could become something disconcertingly dark.

Mendelssohn's later works are less dependent on instantly memorable melody – a fact which some listeners still outspokenly regret – than on structural integration. But that is something for which several composers (think of Verdi, Puccini, Debussy, Stravinsky, Britten) have been criticised in the supposedly more cerebral music they wrote towards the end of their careers.

Texture and harmony are what create its special sound-world, out of which eloquent high violin lines, suggestive of the E minor Violin Concerto, sometimes spring. And if the energy of the first movement of Op. 44, No. 3 lacks the sheer unstoppable momentum of the Octet, that is because Mendelssohn here had other priorities. He needed space for new touches of poignancy, for second thoughts which took longer to express themselves than first ones, and for his continued interest in cyclic form.

He also, or so one would like to think, wanted to celebrate in this work and in its companion pieces his recent happy marriage to the teenage Cécile Jeanrenaud, daughter of the Frankfurt-based minister of the French Reformed Church. Though some people suspected it was her mother he really loved, Mendelssohn's was a cupboard with few skeletons. It was from the composer's elder sister Fanny that Cécile had most to fear. The fact that they did not meet until a year after the wedding speaks for itself.

By the end of their five-month honeymoon, Cécile was pregnant. Their son Carl, who later became a university professor, was the first of five children born at two-year intervals. Clara Schumann's suspicion that the soprano Jenny Lind loved more than Mendelssohn's music was shared by others but remained unproven. Sometimes they strolled along the Rhine together, invariably chaperoned it is said; but, when the composer suffered his fatal stroke, it was with Cécile that he was out walking. She survived him by only six years, dying of tuberculosis at the age of 34.

It is in the scherzo of Op. 44, No. 3 – and Mendelssohn, we should remember, was a specialist in scherzos – that his contentment in the year 1838 could be said to be symbolised. One of the most elaborate specimens of its kind, it possesses not only the gossamer charm he was able to spin with such ease but also an appealingly veiled demureness. It also – and all within the space of four minutes – incorporates a fugato passage introduced by the viola and, as its crowning piece of counterpoint, a double fugue. The comfort of the succeeding *adagio* is shot through with moments of yearning, underpinned by a passionate intensity that prevents the music from ever sounding harmonically sedate.

If the finale sweeps aside the lingering emotion of the slow movement, it never loses the sense of direction that has been present in the music from the start. Ever a champion of circling form, Mendelssohn employs it in this work with fresh subtlety, as all the little resemblances between one movement and another make abundantly clear.

Recordings of Op. 44, No. 3 are not hard to come by, and it is difficult to choose between the Coull Quartet's on the one hand and the Talich

Quartet's on the other. The advantage of the Talich over the Coull, however, is that these fine Czech players compress all three works on to a single CD – and we should remember that the other portions of the triptych are equally worth hearing. Mendelssohn himself had a special affection for the D major, Op. 44, No. 1, shared by the many performers who have come to recognise how beautifully written for the quartet medium it is.

# Fifteen

## 1839
## PIANO TRIO IN D MINOR, OP. 49

Molto allegro ed agitato

Scherzo: Leggiero e vivace

Andante con moto tranquillo

Finale: Allegro assai appassionato

'Sonatas for Piano, which may equally well be played solo, or accompanied by violin and cello' was the cumbersome title of a volume of works produced in 1775 by the most progressive of Bach's sons, Carl Philipp Emanuel. The idea of a piano being 'accompanied' by a violin or cello may seem strange to modern listeners, but for a while it was the norm; and both Haydn and Mozart composed trios in which the piano was dominant, the violin played a subsidiary role, and the cello was largely a passenger.

These were works very different from the trio sonatas of the baroque era, which tended – such are the mysteries of music – to be composed for four instruments, or even for one, but seldom for three. It was Beethoven who established the piano trio as a recognisable equal partnership – and

Schubert, Mendelssohn, Schumann, Brahms and Dvořák all followed suit.

To listen to the Piano Trio in D minor by Mendelssohn – who wrote only two works in the form, as against Haydn's thirty-odd – is to be struck by the power and fullness of the music, which is rather plump and plush by Mendelssohn's own earlier standards, and by how effectively the ideas are shared between the instruments. But by 1839, when Mendelssohn completed this first of his two trios, more than forty years had passed since the heyday of the Haydn trio; and Beethoven, in his 'Ghost' and 'Archduke' trios, had already revealed the dramatic possibilities of the form.

So Mendelssohn was able, without seeming to go over the top, to give the opening theme of the first movement to the cello rather than the piano and, a few bars later, to emancipate the violin, too, in a way which neither Haydn nor Mozart would have dreamed of. While the strings are thus preoccupied with the main theme and its extension, the piano provides a typically agitated – some would say impatient – accompaniment, but it fails to wrest the theme from the other instruments. Indeed, when the second subject arrives, in the form of a sweetly swaying melody for which the term 'second subject' sounds much too formal, it is also allotted first of all to the cello.

This time, however, the piano does succeed in supplying its own song-without-words-like version of what is an attractively sweet Mendelssohn major-key melody. But it never quite gains the initiative in later appearances of the opening theme, where its purpose is mainly to add an air of restlessness – by way of syncopations, hurtling triplets and so forth – to what the strings are playing. Yet the piano's sense of struggle is one of the vital, energising forces of this movement, achieved by Mendelssohn in various ways. Thus, when the recapitulation arrives with the main theme again stated by the cello and with a charming new counter-theme on the violin, the piano suddenly breaks free from the strings with an eloquent little solo cadenza, which briefly slows the pulse of the music, to romantic effect.

But if the piano is deprived of some of the melodic spoils of the first movement, it gains the melodic initiative at the start of the *andante*, written in Mendelssohn's gentlest song-without-words vein. Here, in each section of the music, the piano tends to take the lead before being joined by the strings. With the cello sometimes playing pizzicato, and with the violin sometimes spreading a tender cocoon of tone round the piano part, it is all very delicate; and the same can be said for the succeeding scherzo, decorated in Mendelssohn's most appealing fairy-glitter manner, again with the piano tending to take control but with much sparkling writing for the strings and with some little touches of Mendelssohnian thunder-and-lightning along the way, before the music vanishes in a soft cloud of semiquavers.

As for the finale, charm and pathos rather than more demonstrative moments of passion seem to stamp this *allegro assai appassionato*, which begins with a quietly pattering, poetically Schumannesque main theme and incorporates some mock-strenuous pounding up hill and down dale before the key of D minor is swept aside by the affirmative D major coda. Though this could be meant as some splendid symbolic gesture, reminding us perhaps that Beethoven's Ninth Symphony begins in D minor and ends in D major, it is surely nothing of the kind. Beethoven's grand romantic heroism, in which sunlit major conquers tragic minor, becomes in Mendelssohn's hands more of a make-believe heroism, leading to a characteristically hymnlike close. It may seem less of an achievement; but its aims, after all, were not quite the same.

Performers adore this work, and it is easy to see why. Though requiring consummate technical facility, especially on the part of the pianist, it repays anybody's efforts to convey the peculiar strength of its magic. Martha Argerich, the Argentinian pianist whose international launching pad was the Edinburgh Festival in the 1960s, does it to perfection in her live recording from her own little festival of chamber music, which she started in Lugano in 2002.

Consummate technical facility being one of her many attributes, she drives Renaud and Gautier Capuçon, the brothers who form the rest of the ensemble, at hair-raising speed through the minefield of the scherzo. But the whole performance, coupled with Brahms's F minor Piano Quintet in its magnificent version for two pianos, is a model of what, for all its glitter, boils down to domestic music-making of the most exhilarating sort (EMI Classics 5 57504 2).

One day, no doubt, this will count as a historic performance of Mendelssohn's trio. For a performance which is already historic, try the partnership of Alfred Cortot, Jacques Thibaud and Pablo Casals in their 1927 recording, lovingly renovated by the ever-vigilant Naxos company and available at bargain price (Naxos 8.110185). The coupling is Schumann's tender First Piano Trio, written in the year of Mendelssohn's death and no less responsive to this sort of playing.

# Sixteen

## 1840
## SYMPHONY NO. 2 IN B FLAT MAJOR, OP. 52, 'LOBESGESANG' ('HYMN OF PRAISE')

Sinfonia: Maestoso con moto – Allegro –

Allegretto un poco agitato

Adagio religioso

Allegro moderato maestoso – Allegro di molto –

Recitativo –

A tempo moderato – Andante – Allegro un poco agitato –

Allegro maestoso e molto vivace – Chorale: Andante con moto –

Andante sostenuto assai – Allegro non troppo

At last entering his thirties and speeding towards death, Mendelssohn had identification problems with his Second Symphony, which he resolved, or imagined he did, by describing it as a 'symphony-cantata' and by naming it also his 'Lobesgesang' or 'Hymn of Praise'. In Britain, where it was soon accepted as a pillar of the English Choral Tradition, 'Hymn of Praise' was the title that stuck, and nobody thought of the work as a symphony at all. It was, in any case, quite misleadingly numbered. Not only was it a later work than the 'Italian' symphony (No. 4) and the 'Reformation' (No. 5), but also it interrupted the composition of the 'Scotch' (No. 3), which was begun before but not completed until two years after the 'Hymn of Praise' had had its first performances, under the composer's conductorship, in Leipzig and Birmingham in 1840.

Today, after years of neglect and disparagement, the music looks like regaining some of its old allure. Now that people, rightly or wrongly, are learning to love *Elijah* all over again, the hybrid aspects of the 'Hymn of Praise' are unlikely to impede its progress towards fresh recognition. Yet they remain a disconcerting feature of the work which needs to be faced, even if audiences in general have shown no desire to do so, being happy simply to accept it as it is.

To hail the 'Hymn of Praise' as some sort of Mendelssohnian equivalent of Beethoven's Ninth Symphony is patently ridiculous, though there was a time when enthusiasts did just that. Whatever the structural similarities between the two works – each consists of three orchestral movements followed by a vocal one – Mendelssohn's symphony does not aim at Beethovenian drama. Commissioned for a festival celebrating the quatercentenary of Germany's pioneering printer, Gutenberg, it had aims, as the opening trombone motif brazenly asserts, which were principally ceremonial. But four-square though this opening proclamation sounds, it is put to surprisingly flexible use as the Mendelssohnian 'motto' theme of the entire work. Sometimes, as in the main body of the first movement, it is overworked. But there are so many compensating factors, and such delightful, delicately orchestrated reminiscences of the 'Italian' symphony and other previous inspirations, that the pros far outweigh the cons.

The brooding clarinet solo which links the first movement to the second is in any case a Mendelssohn masterstroke – one of several of this sort – which is worth waiting for. So, for that matter, is the second movement itself, not so much a Mendelssohn scherzo as a sort of Venetian waltz in G minor, if such a thing can be imagined, with curious hints of Berlioz (whose music Mendelssohn condemned) and foretastes of Tchaikovsky, not least in its tangy blend of oboe and bassoon tone. In the middle section, a characteristic piece of Mendelssohn legerdemain, the 'motto' theme is transformed into a chorale while the waltz continues to revolve in counterpoint. As a combination of the sacred and the secular, it is one of his most captivating inspirations.

Admirers of the slow movement of the 'Scotch' symphony will not fail to spot how much the *adagio religioso* here resembles that other, more familiar, *adagio*. If it sounds rather more subdued, and rather less expressive, that is probably because it is meant to be simply an intermezzo before the long finale – fully half the length of the entire work – enters with the motto theme and the first sound of the chorus singing words from the Lutheran Bible, which Brahms would employ later in his *German*

*Requiem*. Thereafter, the voices of two sopranos and a tenor are infiltrated, sometimes very strikingly, into the choral and orchestral texture.

The music is now heading towards the famous 'watchman' scene which, with its question 'Will the night soon pass?', was once thought to be the work's main *raison d'être* (it was reputedly inspired by a sleepless night suffered by Mendelssohn himself). The soprano response and the succeeding chorus, 'The night is gone', clearly symbolise Gutenberg's achievement as a printer; and from here on, with occasional flavourings of Bach to remind us that it was Mendelssohn who rediscovered the *St Matthew Passion*, the music moves steadily to its contrapuntal climax and final statement of the motto theme.

Alas, like the First Symphony, the Second suffers from a dearth of really good modern recordings. What the music needs is a bracing, period-conscious performance of the sort you might expect to hear from John Eliot Gardiner, if his recordings of the 'Reformation' and 'Italian' symphonies are anything to go by. What it gets is the blandness of Karajan, Haitink, Dohnanyi, Masur, Ashkenazy and various others, though Claudio Abbado's performance, drawn from his complete set with the London Symphony Orchestra, has enough personality to hold the attention (DG 423 143-2).

By far the most interesting performance, however, comes from the far less famous combination of Christoph Spering and Das Neue Orchester ('The New Orchestra') on the obscure but valuable Opus 111 label

(Op. 30-98). Here we encounter a keen-edged stylishness conspicuously missing from the other performances, which, in comparison, sound very generalised. The soloists, including the young Finnish soprano, Soile Isokoski, sing as a team, with such sweetness of tone that the work is placed in new and refreshing perspective. The Musicus Köln Chorus, another unknown quantity, turns out to be one more vital factor in the performance's success.

# Seventeen

## 1842
## SYMPHONY NO. 3 IN A MINOR, OP. 56 ('SCOTCH')

Andante con moto – Allegro un poco agitato –       Vivace non troppo –

Adagio –                    Allegro vivacissimo – Allegro maestoso assai


When the ailing 38-year-old Chopin toured Scotland in 1848, a year after Mendelssohn's death, the coach journey and the weather nearly killed him. But the 20-year-old Mendelssohn, in 1829, suffered nothing worse than seasickness on his journey to the Hebrides, and his Scottish tour turned out to be the most productive of its kind ever undertaken by a visiting composer.

Holyrood Palace in Edinburgh was his inspirational starting point, giving him the opening notes of his 'Scotch' symphony, which was the nickname he chose in nineteenth-century preference to what modern Scots would insist on calling *Scottish*. Most of the time, however, he was happy to refer to it simply as his Symphony in A minor, and he left a vivid description of its moment of conception. It happened, he romantically remarked, on an evening visit to where Mary Queen of Scots had 'lived and loved'. The chapel, he noted, had lost its roof and was overgrown with grass and ivy. The altar at which Mary was crowned Queen of Scotland was broken. 'Everything', he reported, 'was in ruins, decayed and open to the skies. I believe I found there today the beginning of my "Scotch" symphony.'

The actual writing of the work, however, did not begin until some years later in Rome, by which time he was also composing his 'Italian' symphony and was having problems finding his way back into his 'Scottish fog mood'. Since both works are in the same key – the 'Scotch' in A minor moving into A major, the 'Italian' in A major moving into A minor – it seems possible that he sometimes found it hard to differentiate between them. Certainly, there are moments when the quick marching finale of the 'Scotch' symphony sounds on the brink of transforming itself into the whirling saltarello which ends the 'Italian'.

Schumann, as one of the most distinguished critics of his day, certainly got the two works confused in his mind. In his review of the 'Scotch' symphony in the *Neue Zeitschrift für Musik*, he paid special tribute to the 'old tunes of lovely Italy' contained therein. Folk tunes, in fact, are just what both symphonies lack – Mendelssohn had no enthusiasm for them, the Scottish ones in particular being associated by him with men with 'long red beards, tartan plaids, bonnets and feathers, naked knees, and their bagpipes in their hands'.

True, in the scherzo of the 'Scotch', clarinet and strings create a sprightly evocation of the kind of music Mendelssohn might have heard on his Scottish tour. But, though 'Charlie is my Darling' is often cited as its source, the composer probably arrived at the peculiarly Scottish-sounding melody all by himself, ensuring that it carried a thoroughly Mendelssohnian stamp. His hatred of Scottish traditional music, it turned out, was surpassed only by his loathing of Welsh.

So what is actually Scottish about the 'Scotch' symphony? The slow introduction to the first movement may seem to some listeners – if not to Schumann – to have a characteristic dourness (Mendelssohn said that to all questions he asked in Scotland he got a dry 'no' in reply). It seems apt that an amended version of the opening theme, under the title 'Bad Weather', found its way into his *Erste Walpurgisnacht* ('First Walpurgis Night'), music on which he was simultaneously at work.

This theme casts its shadow over the entire symphony, inspiring the two main subjects of the first movement's *allegro* section and being hinted at later in the 'Charlie is my Darling' theme of the exhilaratingly nimble scherzo, which is not structured like a Beethovenian scherzo and trio but is a more elaborate movement in sonata form. It is also heard in a glowing, rather grandiose A major version ('Better Weather'?) as the climax of the finale, filled with whooping horns.

There was a time when this sonorous ending was thought to have been arbitrarily tacked on, in order to bring the symphony – Mendelssohn's last to be completed, even if its number suggests otherwise – to a triumphant close in a way that would please its dedicatee, his friend 'Queen Victoria of Great Britain and Ireland'. But in fact this coda, which Mendelssohn said should be suggestive of the sound of a men's chorus, is one of the symphony's many unifying features, prompting Schumann (rightly this time) to speak of the 'homogeneity of all four movements'.

The placid – some would say saccharine – main theme of the preceding slow movement, on the other hand, may seem to belong to a different world entirely; but its Scottish sentimentality, if that is what it is, is not overpressed. The second theme of this *adagio* harks back, at least in mood, to the sombre unifying music of the start of the work. Nor, in spite of what could be called its Victorian chastity, does this meditative movement lack a climax. Meditation gradually gives way to march. Brass and drums invade the texture. An army, or so it would seem, is on the move.

Though the music soon calms down again, the military aspect does not retreat. It resumes, softly but excitedly, in the form of a forced march at the start of the finale. The fact that this *allegro vivacissimo* is described on the title page as an *allegro guerriero* (meaning a 'warlike' allegro) speaks for itself. Yet this is not, on the whole, bellicose music. Mendelssohn's troops are conspicuously light-footed, indeed positively dancing; and the way the pulse begins to slow and the action to dwindle just before the coda is pure and very typical Mendelssohnian poetry.

This exceptional delicacy of touch – which is what, for some people, can make the coda, when it abruptly arrives, seem so disappointingly pompous – is one of the factors that transform the work into a master-piece. The point, it's true, is often missed by big symphony orchestras and the star conductors who want to 'make something out of' the 'Scotch' symphony.

In its avoidance of such an approach, the Scottish Chamber Orchestra's millennial recording of the work, made in the Usher Hall, Edinburgh, is greatly refreshing. Joseph Swensen, as conductor, seizes his chance to capture all the deftness and luminosity for which the music cries out. Fine woodwind detail, especially (but not only) the important clarinet part, never gets lost in the string tone. Structurally coherent, and observant of the composer's desire for only the shortest of pauses between movements, the performance also conveys the music as a series of studies in naturalism – which, here and in *The Hebrides*, was one of Mendelssohn's special achievements. A talented landscape painter in his spare time, he knew how to paint landscapes in music.

Yet there is muscle in Swensen's conducting where it is needed, as in the first movement's *Flying Dutchman*-like climax. A year ahead of Wagner, who vilified Mendelssohn but knew how to filch from him, the music lets you hear the nordic wind and feel the nordic spray. There is also a Berliozian poetry – strikingly underlined by Swensen – in the way the pace decelerates immediately afterwards, bringing to the end of the movement a dreamlike quality reminiscent of the equivalent passage in the first movement of the *Symphonie Fantastique*.

The scherzo is sprightly, the *adagio* never sugared, the finale mercurial and catlike in its tread. In the coda, there is no hint of bombast. In comparison, most other recordings of this work sound distinctly overweight. The well-filled disc, which incorporates *The Hebrides* overture and the Violin Concerto, adds up to an exemplary Mendelssohn concert (Linn CKD 205).

For those who fancy a traditionally bigger-boned performance, there are plenty of options. Peter Maag's classic recording with the London Symphony Orchestra has stood the test of time, the conductor perhaps finding some emotional link between his native Switzerland and Mendelssohn's Scotland. Excerpts from *A Midsummer Night's Dream*, recorded as long ago as 1957, complete this desirable disc (Decca ADD 466 990-2). Among recordings which couple the 'Scotch' with the 'Italian', Abbado's with the LSO (DG 427 810-2) and Norrington's with the London Classical Players (Virgin 5 61735-2) remain strong recommendations.

# Eighteen

## 1844
## VIOLIN CONCERTO IN E MINOR, OP 64

Allegro molto appassionato –                                      Andante

Allegretto non troppo – Allegro molto vivace


No composer, not even Rossini in his childhood string sonatas, has written with such instant ease as Mendelssohn, and nobody, not even Mozart, to such conscientious purpose. No matter how often it is said, it is a truth which has to be reiterated, if only to stress that the tiredness which hit him in his thirties did not damage his genius. For those who insist that the boy genius had begun to repeat himself, just one work needs to be mentioned as evidence of this untruth: the famous Violin Concerto in E minor, completed in 1844 when he was 35, and filled with music of maturity, not decline.

By then, of his own volition, he had opened the great Leipzig conservatoire, with himself as head of piano and ensemble studies and his friend Robert Schumann in charge of piano and composition. With teachers as renowned as these, and with the gifted Niels Gade from Denmark as protégé, there was little wonder that would-be composers and performers from all over Europe applied – and continued to apply – to study there, with Grieg (after Mendelssohn's death) working so hard during his Leipzig period that he permanently damaged his health.

But then, the same could be said for Mendelssohn himself. At the time of the conservatoire's opening, he was already one of the most celebrated conductors in Europe, constantly in demand in England and facing up to his heavy responsibilities as director of the Leipzig Gewandhaus Orchestra, whose leader, Ferdinand David, was the great Joseph Joachim's teacher.

Joachim himself played Mendelssohn's Violin Concerto in Dresden at the age of 14 with Schumann as conductor, but it was for David – principal violin teacher at the conservatory – that the work was written, and it was David who gave the composer much practical advice during the concerto's surprisingly long (by Mendelssohn's standards) gestation period. This lasted six years and continued after the official premiere, which was conducted by young Gade, the composer himself being too exhausted to do so. The feverish activity of his career was taking its toll. He was suffering from alarming headaches and was increasingly aware that he would have to reduce his workload. 'What is not done today is done tomorrow, and there is leisure for everything', he declared hopefully. It was not the sort of thing he would have said a few years earlier.

Yet never has a concerto had a more illustrious send-off than Mendelssohn's, or has seemed to spring more intact from the pen of its creator. Its abundant melodies sound totally spontaneous and instantly memorable – their problem today is that their sheer familiarity, in all but the best performances, can make them sound tarnished and open to accusations of superficiality. But superficial they are not. Even their apparent ease did not come easily to their composer, and we should rejoice that the machinery of the concerto – the way one splendid tune works up to a climax before leading to another, the poise of the accompaniments, the beauty of the transition passages, the control of tension and relaxation – operates so discreetly and naturally, as if the concerto were composed in a single sweep. This, however, was not the case. As Mendelssohn himself reported, the opening notes in E minor kept spinning in his head, giving him no peace, and impeding the progress of the rest of the work. Such is the mystery of genius.

The first movement, in a manner typical of its composer, manages to be both passionate and delicate, yet its smooth flow does not conceal some incomparable strokes of inspiration, such as the soloist's sustaining of a long low G while the woodwind announce the exquisite *tranquillo* second subject. The placing of the cadenza, before instead of after the recapitulation of the principal themes, is a startling moment of surprise. Who could ever describe Mendelssohn as unoriginal? Yet the surprise has been scrupulously prepared, the music is deliberately allowed to lose momentum, as if to suggest that the recapitulation is pending. Instead, it is the cadenza which sidles in.

No less surprising, and more easily spotted by listeners not versed in musical structure, is the way the first movement's fast, impulsive coda is propelled straight into the slow movement by way of a note suspended on the bassoon, followed by the most gentle of modulations on the strings until the concerto settles iridescently in the key of simple C major. Though given no more than the one-word marking, *andante*, the music has no lack of sweet expressiveness, either in the serenity of its main theme or in what sounds like the quiet anguish of the middle section before the theme returns.

Recognising that a straight move to the scurrying wit of the finale might seem too abrupt, the ever-thoughtful Mendelssohn inserted – at a late date in the composition? – a little interlude, poetically recalling the start of the first movement and directed to be played 'not too fast'. It is another moment of Mendelssohn magic, in which, while touchingly evoking what has previously been heard, the soloist prepares us for the new mood and the new key of E major. Then the music dashes off into a new array of mercurial melodies, not all of them easy to articulate with the essential lightness of touch, but filled with the magic of *A Midsummer Night's Dream*. One of the best of them, on the cellos, is held back until fairly late in the movement, but serves to remind us once again of Mendelssohn's tirelessly spinning invention.

# NOTES ON MENDELSSOHN

To record Mendelssohn's Violin Concerto is almost every violinist's desire, and most of the great soloists from Heifetz onwards have done so. Heifetz's wonderfully articulated performance, indeed, leads the pack, its sound quality remarkably good for its age, the Tchaikovsky Violin Concerto a perfect coupling (RCA 09026 61743-2). If you want a star name, your options include Joshua Bell, Kyung-Wha Chung, Nigel Kennedy, Yehudi Menuhin, Nathan Milstein, Anne-Sophie Mutter, Itzhak Perlman, Isaac Stern and (with a luminous warmth of tone) Josef Suk.

This critic's choice, however, would be a more recent contender, the Russian Viktoria Mullova, who employs gut strings and a searching sense of Mendelssohnian style in tribute to authenticity, yet loses nothing in terms of virtuosity or tonal sweetness. With John Eliot Gardiner and his Orchestre Révolutionnaire et Romantique placing her performance in the right period context, here is a recording which throws the freshest of light upon the music and includes Beethoven's Violin Concerto as a generous bonus (Philips 473 872-2).

# Nineteen

## 1845
## STRING QUINTET No. 2 IN B FLAT MAJOR, Op. 87

Allegro vivace                              Andante scherzando

Adagio e lento                          Allegro molto vivace


Mendelssohn authorities traditionally dismiss this little-known master-piece, dating from near the end of his career, as no more than a rerun of his spectacularly inspired string Octet, written at the beginning. But, even if it amounted to no more than that, it would still be worth hearing, not least for the way it compresses the sound of eight instruments into that of five. But in fact it is much more than an attempt to repeat an old success, and it is the work's sometimes disorientating links with its brilliant predecessor which prove the point.

Far from representing a burnt-out composer's desire to regain lost glory, Mendelssohn's Second String Quintet takes the panache of the

Octet as its starting point but employs it to quite different ends. At the age of 36, Mendelssohn was in any case a different man. No longer the *wunderkind* who magicked everything he touched, he was now the victim of seriously deteriorating stamina. His temper was shorter, his mood-swings alarming. His wide-ranging responsibilities as composer, conductor, teacher, administrator and family man were overstretching his abilities. Instead of travelling less, he was travelling more. Wise after the event, we can see that he was clearly heading – with the death of his sister in May 1847 as a dreadful trigger – towards the stroke that killed him in the November of that year.

True, it is hard to think of Mendelssohn – seemingly the most equable of men, whom Bernard Shaw would later describe as the epitome of 'kid-glove gentility' – in quite that way. But the evidence is there to be examined. Not for nothing did his doctor tell him to slow down. The blinding headaches and attacks of vertigo (one of them while standing on a bridge looking at the Thames) from which he was suffering spoke for themselves. Yet he was unable to relax or reduce his punishing schedule.

The turmoil of the mature Mendelssohn's mind, and the nervous strain, may not be reflected in all his music of the period (he celebrated the ninth of his ten visits to Britain with the splendour of *Elijah* in 1846); but their undercurrents are audible. And they can certainly be heard in the first movement of the B flat Quintet, which spurts off with all the spitfire vitality of the youthful Octet but soon shows signs of almost manic emotional stress. Again and again, exuberance escalates into what sounds like dangerously strenuous passion; and the first violin line, set against agitated tremolandi from the other instruments (including the extra viola which Mozart had added to the conventional string quartet in order to intensify the light and shade of his string quintets) has a kind of feverish nerviness very different from the sweetness of the E minor Violin Concerto of the previous year.

The succeeding *andante scherzando* – slow movement or scherzo? – extinguishes the fires of the first movement and replaces them with an intermezzo filled with Mendelssohnian ambiguity. Its gait is that of a graceful but slightly faltering dance, which moves stealthily and spectrally through its paces with pizzicato effects but none of the sparkle of Mendelssohn's more celebrated scherzos.

Elfin charm, on this evidence, is a thing of the past, and the ferocity of the genuine slow movement, which follows, confirms the fact. Here we reach the emotional heart of the work, and one of the rare moments when Mendelssohn's self-control is allowed to break down. From the funereal opening bars – an anticipation of his own and Fanny's fate? – the music moves through passages of increasing tension and disruption until the first violin, with shudders from the other instruments, brings it to a high-pitched, almost operatic climax.

Though the movement ends surprisingly peacefully, something more is needed to restore a sense of B flat major well-being, and the finale tries hard to provide it. It may not be Mendelssohn's greatest finale, any more than the comic finale of Beethoven's penultimate quartet, the B flat major, Op. 130, was Beethoven's. Nevertheless, in its determined energy, it does the trick. To make its point, it needs to be performed with total commitment – but that is a quality required by the work as a whole.

Its challenge, however, is something to which ensembles seldom bother to respond. String quartets must recruit an extra player in order to perform it, and when they do so they usually end by opting for Mozart. Recordings are likewise few and far between, but nobody need look beyond the Raphael Ensemble's characteristically excellent disc, which has the merit of including the much earlier Quintet in A major, Op. 18, as coupling (Hyperion CDA 66993).

These British players are experts in the quintet and sextet repertoire, and the Quintet in B flat is presented with vibrant persuasiveness. The two works hold a position in Mendelssohn's output akin to that of the *Midsummer Night's Dream* overture, written at 17, and the incidental music which followed seventeen years later. But whereas in the incidental music he deliberately thought his way back into his boyhood style, his genius in the quintets had no such fetters. Amid the elegance of Op. 18, the extra viola adds a sinister timbre to the featherweight scherzo. In Op. 87, the even sharper chiaroscuro is highlighted by the performance to powerful effect.

# Twenty

## 1847
## STRING QUARTET IN F MINOR, OP. 80

Allegro vivace assai – Presto

Adagio

Allegro assai

Finale: Allegro molto

Mendelssohn can no longer be described as a tragic case of dwindling genius, his best works written while he was still a teenager, his worst ones dating from the last years of his brief life. Today, you have to dislike him and his music rather a lot to say something like that. Those who adore him – and, as we have again come to recognise more than 150 years after he fell from grace, there is plenty about him to adore – would prefer to argue that there are no 'worst' works, only works some of which are less inspired than others. The F minor Quartet, written just before his death, is not such a one. It is a masterpiece very different from, but quite the equal of, the brilliant, carefree Octet for strings, that early outburst of genius by which the rest of his output was unfortunately destined to be judged.

Why, then, are people only now beginning to perceive its greatness? Partly, no doubt, because almost nobody knows it, but also because by Mendelssohn standards it can sound unpolished, perhaps even unfinished, and thus one more work by this composer which has failed to fulfil its potential. In the pedantic words of Philip Radcliffe, the composer's British *Master Musicians* biographer: 'Regarded purely as quartet writing, this is not a good work'. From such biographers do many great composers suffer. But though Mendelssohn was undoubtedly dying when he wrote his last quartet, he had by no means run out of musical steam. If the music sounded unpolished, or even (as another commentator has put it) 'ugly', that was how it was meant to sound.

Ugliness, after all, was a quality Mendelssohn was perfectly capable of remedying if he wished. He was an expert in the art of musical urbanity. The point about the F minor Quartet, however, was that he did not want it to be merely beautiful. His beloved sister Fanny had just died suddenly of a stroke at the age of 41 while directing a Berlin rehearsal of *Die erste Walpurgisnacht* (another mature Mendelssohn masterpiece whose greatness remains unappreciated). On hearing the news, the composer collapsed. His last quartet – his 'Requiem for Fanny' – was destined to be the expression of an anguish from which he never fully recovered. While attempting to recuperate at Interlaken, among the Swiss lakes which Brahms would later find so inspirational, he was described by his friend Henry Chorley as looking 'aged and sad, and stooped more than I had ever before seen him do'. He was only 38 years old.

Visiting Fanny's home in Berlin soon after completing his desolate instrumental elegy in her memory, he found it just as it had been when she was alive. Once again he suffered an emotional collapse, which led all too speedily to his own fatal brain haemorrhage. The portents of this were already present in the pulsating passion of the quartet, with its feverishly hurtling opening notes, its first high violin entry like a scream of pain, and its dangerously unrelieved intensity of expression. An anger of a supposedly quite un-Mendelssohnian sort pervades the first movement, in which the music races into its coda with unprecedented fury.

But Mendelssohn, far from being as placid as people have been taught to believe, was quite often an angry man. The succeeding scherzo, or what in this case should be called an anti-scherzo, screws up the tension still further. The equestrian rhythm suggests some sort of ride to the abyss. The trio section is as grim as a midnight death rattle. Only in the slow movement is a mood of wintry consolation allowed to intrude; but it is swept aside by the restlessness of the finale, swinging between explosiveness and moments of hushed despair.

If Mendelssohn had survived this state of pre-Mahlerish angst, would he have entered, before he was 40, a new, different, startling period of inspiration? How would the recent composer of *Elijah* have adjusted, if at all, to the death of his sister? How would the man posthumously accused by Bernard Shaw of 'oratorio-mongering' have coped with the death, not long afterwards, of his young wife?

Such questions have been asked before. A good performance of this quartet – which would mean a performance confirming that this is music not only 'terse' and 'implosive' but also 'inscribed with Mendelssohn's anger', as Paul Driver of the *Sunday Times* put it in an appreciative review of a survey of Mendelssohn's chamber music in Manchester in 2003 – surely supplies the answer. On that occasion, as Driver reported, the task was 'savagely undertaken' by the Endellion Quartet, one of the impressive bands of British-based ensembles who, towards the end of the twentieth century, showed themselves to be worthy successors of the great Amadeus Quartet.

The Coull Quartet, on the evidence of its complete recording of Mendelssohn's quartets, is clearly another, capable of unleashing the full torrent of the first movement of Op. 80 and sustaining the rest of the work with no loss of tension (Hyperion CDS 44051/3). As the performance demonstrates, the music may be 'classical' in format but the result breaks all the rules of classical decorum – which must be why, to some ears, Op. 80 sounds an ugly work.

The Aurora Quartet's performance forms part of another excellent complete set, whose components, at bargain price, can be bought separately. Op. 80 comes coupled with Op. 44, No. 1 and two of the four fragments for quartet, Op. 81 – a particularly inviting assembly, played with ample ardour (Naxos 8.550861). Best of all, perhaps, is the Talich Quartet's more recent performance, completing this fine Czech ensemble's survey of these works. By contrasting this uncontrolled outburst of grief with the self-disciplined yet never academic music of the very early E flat major Quartet, composed at the age of 14, the Talichs are clearly making a point. It is up to us to decide what it is.

*On 4 November 1847, after a series of ever-worsening strokes, Mendelssohn died in Leipzig, over whose Gewandhaus concerts he had reigned for twelve years. In his funeral procession, Robert Schumann was among the pall-bearers, just as Franz Schubert had been a torch-bearer at Beethoven's. For two days, hundreds of mourners kept vigil beside the open coffin. After a service in the Paulinerkirche, ending with the final chorus from Bach's* St Matthew Passion, *the coffin was taken by special train to Berlin, where thousands of people followed the hearse. The casket, it was said, looked like an 'island of peace amid a surging crowd'. Mendelssohn was buried in the Trinity Cemetery close to the grave of his sister Fanny, whose death five months earlier had seemed to have so much bearing on his own.*

*Further services were held soon afterwards in Vienna, Paris, London and New York. Three years later, the influential* Neue Zeitschrift für Musik *said of Mendelssohn that 'he was not able, even one single time, to call forth in us that deep, heart-searching effect which we await from art'. The anonymous author of the article was Richard Wagner, who notoriously allowed Mendelssohn's Jewishness to influence his response to music which he had previously been willing to learn from. But others, too, turned against Mendelssohn, and not only for anti-semitic reasons. He was a classic example of the composer who, feted in his lifetime, is despised after death.*

*Would he have been as interesting to meet as Mozart? Almost certainly not, and therein perhaps lies a major difference between the two men. Yet today, once again, it is easy to revere him, and the repertoire is all the better for containing more Mendelssohn now than at any period since his lifetime.*

# FURTHER READING

Rudolf Elvers (ed.), *Felix Mendelssohn: A Life in Letters* (Cassell, 1986; Fromm International, 1986)

Mendelssohn was an excellent letter-writer, just as he was excellent at everything else that mattered to him. These ones form an illuminating and witty semi-autobiography, expertly translated by Craig Tomlinson.

Peter Mercer-Taylor, *The Life of Mendelssohn* (Cambridge, 2000)

For readers with limited patience, this is the one to buy – a good, well-written, up-to-date short life, with plenty of relevant anecdotes and enough information about the music, and sound enough judgements, to satisfy hasty readers.

Philip Radcliffe, *The Master Musicians: Mendelssohn* (Dent, 1967; Oxford, 2001)

Though sufficiently up to date to mention the string symphonies and other twentieth-century discoveries, this irritating book now rather shows its age, not least in its schoolmasterly attitude to works deserving admiration rather than niggling criticism.

# NOTES ON MENDELSSOHN

Charles Rosen, *The Romantic Generation* (HarperCollins, 1996)

Mendelssohn in the context of Schubert, Meyerbeer, Schumann, Liszt, Bellini, Chopin and Berlioz. Full of perceptions and written with highly readable intelligence.

R. Larry Todd, *Mendelssohn: A Life in Music* (Oxford, 2003)

At last, the Mendelssohn life and works we have been waiting for. A big, detailed study running to more than 700 pages, it gets in everything that matters but never grows dull. Like other academic experts, Todd can be a little sniffy about works which deserve to be championed. In this respect, his vigorously defensive preface promises more than it delivers, but on the whole there is little to fault and much to praise in this thoroughly modern biography.

# GLOSSARY

**Adagio**. Italian term for 'slow', often interpreted as very slow. But can also mean 'comfortable'.

**Affettuoso**. Italian term for 'with feeling'.

**Agitato**. Italian term for 'agitated'.

**Allegro**. Italian term for 'light' or 'fast'. But is an 'allegretto' (meaning, literally, 'a little allegro') slower or faster than allegro? The term is usually accepted as meaning slower, but is irritatingly ambiguous.

**Andante**. Italian term for 'at walking pace'.

**Andantino**. Irritatingly ambiguous Italian term, usually taken to mean a little faster than andante, but which can also be interpreted as a little slower than andante.

**Appassionato**. Italian term for 'impassioned'.

**Aria**. Italian term for 'air' or 'song', particularly in an opera.

**Arpeggio**. Split chord, i.e. a chord whose notes are spread in a harplike manner instead of being sounded simultaneously.

**Assai**. Italian term for 'very'.

**Ballade**. Instrumental piece in the style of (or with reference to) a sung ballade.

**Baritone**. Singer whose voice range lies between that of a tenor and a bass.

**Cadenza**. Solo passage of varying length, particularly in the first movement of a concerto or in a vocal work, enabling the soloist to display his/her technique in an improvisational manner relevant to the work being performed. Mendelssohn tended to write down his own cadenzas.

**Canon**. Passage in which a melody performed by one instrument or voice is taken up by another before the previous voice has finished.

**Cantabile**. Italian term for 'in a singing manner'.

**Cantata**. A vocal work, often but not necessarily of a religious nature, usually involving solo voices and chorus with orchestra.

**Canzonetta**. Light Italian song. The term is also used for orchestral or instrumental movements in the style of such a song.

**Cavatina**. A song, or songlike instrumental piece, usually rather slow.

**Chamber orchestra**. Smallish orchestra, usually of up to about forty players, suitable for performing in surroundings more intimate than a large concert hall. Though chamber orchestras have their own established repertoire, symphony orchestras frequently intrude on it, just as chamber orchestras today increasingly invade the symphony orchestra's territory, often with conspicuous, indeed revelatory, success, especially in the case of Mendelssohn's music.

**Chiaroscuro**. The effect of light and dark imagery in a painting.

**Chromatic**. Put simply, a scale which moves in semitones or, in piano terms, one which uses all the black notes as well as the white notes of the keyboard. Chromatic harmony is thus richer than diatonic harmony, which involves only the notes of the normal major or minor scales.

**Coda**. Italian term for 'tail' or 'tailpiece'. The closing section of a movement, often dramatically expanded by Beethoven and by Mendelssohn in the finale of his 'Scotch' symphony.

**Con brio**. Italian term for 'with spirit'.

**Concerto**. In Mendelssohn's time, a work for solo instrument (or instruments) and orchestra, involving dramatic contrasts and instrumental repartee. Mendelssohn's most famous work in the form is his Violin Concerto in E minor.

**Con fuoco**. Italian term meaning 'with fire'.

**Con moto**. Italian term for 'with motion'.

**Counterpoint**. The combination of two or more melodies or musical figures in such a way that they make musical sense.

**Dactylic**. Metre based on the repetition of one long beat followed by two shorter ones.

**Dominant**. The fifth note of the scale. For example, the dominant of the scale of C is the note G, which is four notes above C.

**Espressivo**. Italian term for 'expressive'.

**Fantasy**. A mood piece of some sort, free-ranging and (at least seemingly) improvisational in style. In Bach's day, a fantasy tended to be an elaborate and contrapuntal keyboard piece, often for organ. Later composers, including Mendelssohn, responded to this precedent in their own way. Alternative spelling: Phantasie.

**Finale**. The concluding movement of a work (e.g. symphony, string quartet, sonata) in several movements.

**Fortissimo**. Italian term for 'very loud'. Abbreviated to *ff* in musical terminology.

**Fugato**. Passage in fugal style incorporated in an orchestral, instrumental or choral work.

**Fugue**. A type of composition, movement, or section of a movement involving a given number of instruments or voices which enter separately, at different pitches, in imitation of each other.

**Intégrale**. French term for a complete and integrated series of performances of a particular type of work by a single composer, e.g. Mendelssohn's string quartets.

**Intermezzo**. Italian word for 'interlude'. Type of movement favoured by Mendelssohn as a slower-moving alternative to scherzo.

**Larghetto**. Italian term for 'slow and dignified'.

**Leggiero**. Italian term for 'lightly'.

**Maestoso**. Italian term for 'majestic'.

**Minuet**. Dance in triple-time, usually employed as the second or third movement of a string quartet, or the third movement of a symphony. The contrasted middle section of a minuet is known as a trio, because there was a tradition for writing it in three-part harmony.

**Moderato**. Italian term for 'at moderate speed'.

**Molto**. Italian term for 'very'.

**Mosso**. Italian term for 'animated'.

**Motto**, or **motto theme**. A recurring theme, which can have considerable structural importance in the symphonic and chamber music of Mendelssohn's time. Mendelssohn was one of the great pioneers of motto themes, which Wagner employed as 'leitmotifs' in his music dramas.

**Non tardante**. Italian term meaning 'without slowing up'.

**Non troppo**. Italian term for 'not too much'.

**Opera**. Music drama or 'sung play', in which the cast sing their roles rather than speak them – though speech is employed in some operas, including, most expressively, Beethoven's *Fidelio*. A vital component of opera is the orchestra, providing far more than a mere accompaniment, with a chorus, large or small, supplying another (though not essential) dramatic dimension. Opera as we know it was born in Italy around 1600, spreading to France, Germany, Austria and other countries, and inspiring many cities to build their own opera houses for its performance. It was not a form, however, to which Mendelssohn felt greatly attracted, though his oratorio *Elijah* has been described as an opera in disguise.

**Overture**. Orchestral prelude to an opera. Beethoven composed four overtures for *Fidelio*, as well as various 'concert' overtures designed for separate performance in a concert hall. Self-sufficient concert overtures form an important feature of Mendelssohn's output.

**Pianissimo**. Italian term for 'very soft'. Pianissimo passages – or entire movements – are a special feature of Mendelssohn's music. Abbreviated to *pp* in musical terminology.

**Piano trio**. From Haydn's time onwards, a work usually written for piano, violin, and cello.

**Pizzicato**. Plucked note on a string instrument.

**Prestissimo**. Italian term for 'as fast as possible'.

**Presto**. Italian term for 'fast', often taken to mean as fast as possible (which would in fact be prestissimo).

**Quartet**. Work for four instruments, or ensemble specialising in the performance of such a work. The art of the string quartet (two violins, viola and cello) was perfected by Haydn, who influenced (and was influenced by) Mozart. The form was developed and expanded by Beethoven, whose sixteen quartets form a major portion of his output, and by Mendelssohn, whose quartets are similarly crucial works.

**Recitavo**. Italian term for 'recitative'. Delamatory passage for voice, usually preceding an aria. But music in the style of a recitative can also be found in orchestral or instrumental works.

**Rondo form**. Italian term for what was traditionally the spirited finale of a symphony, string quartet or sonata. The word refers to the fact that the opening theme or section of the movement keeps recurring, or coming 'round' again, thereby forming an essential part of the music's structure. Slow movements can also be in rondo form.

**Saltarello**. Fast Italian dance, usually in 6/8 time, originating in the sixteenth century. The finale of Mendelssohn's 'Italian' symphony is in the style of such a dance.

**Scherzando**. In the manner of a scherzo (see below).

**Scherzo**. Italian term for 'joke'. Title applied by Beethoven, and to a lesser extent by Haydn, to what until then had been a movement in the form of a minuet. In Beethoven's hands, scherzos replaced minuets in symphonies, string quartets, trios and sonatas. They were generally faster, more volatile and often (though not necessarily) humorous. Mendelssohn's scherzos are famously sparkling, light-footed, elfin, keenly characterised and sometimes sinister.

**Semplice**. Italian term for 'simple'.

**Sonata**. A work for one or two instruments, usually consisting of three or four carefully structured and contrasted movements.

**Sonata form**. Term describing the structure of what was usually the first movement of a sonata during Mozart's period and later. Put simply, it consisted of an 'exposition', based on two or more contrasted themes, a 'development' section in which the material already heard is altered, developed, broken up or tautened in various ways, a 'recapitulation' in which the introductory material is assembled in something like its original form, and a 'coda' or tailpiece, which rounds the music off or brings it to some sort of closing climax.

**Soprano**. The highest female voice, ranging from middle C upwards.

**Sostenuto**. Italian term for 'sustained'.

**Staccato**. Italian term for 'short and detached', much used by Mendelssohn. Opposite of *legato*, meaning smooth. Signified by a dot over the printed note.

**Symphony**. Form of orchestral work in several movements, usually of an ambitious nature. Much favoured by Haydn (known as the 'father of the symphony'), Mozart, Beethoven, Schubert, Mendelssohn, Brahms and their successors.

**Symphony orchestra**. Orchestra designed to perform symphonies and similar works, with enough players to meet the music's demands. Though Haydn and Mozart visualised the use of big orchestras, their works are elucidated more satisfactorily by small ones, now known as chamber orchestras. The development in the size and firepower of the symphony orchestra took place in the nineteenth century, partly through the extra instruments required by Beethoven's Fifth and Ninth symphonies and the music's dramatic demands, and also through the increasing size of concert halls. But size is not everything, and the sound of the 'Eroica' symphony played by a chamber orchestra in a smallish hall can be more startling and enthralling than that of the same work played by a big orchestra in larger surroundings.

**Tenor**. High male voice, employed by Mozart and Beethoven in operatic and choral works and by Mendelssohn in his oratorios.

**Tonic**. The keynote of a scale. For example, the keynote of the scale of C is the note C.

**Tremolo**. Italian term for 'trembling'. The rapid 'trembling' repetition of a single note, or alternation between two notes.

**Trill**. Musical term for the rapid alternation of the written note and the note above. Trills are traditionally decorative, but in keyboard terms they are a way of sustaining the sound of a note.

**Trio**. A word with several musical meanings: (1) a work for three instruments, (2) the ensemble which performs such a work, and (3) the name of the middle section of a minuet or scherzo, so called because at one time it was written in three-part harmony. Mendelssohn's trios are for piano, violin and cello, a format perfected by Beethoven and generally known as a piano trio.

**Triplet**. A group of three notes of equal duration, written where some other quantity of notes (perhaps just a single note) is implied by the time signature.

**Vibrato**. Italian term for the 'rapid vibration' in pitch produced by instrumentalists or singers in their performance of a piece of music. Exaggerated vibrato is often described, disparagingly, as 'wobble'. As the history of the symphony orchestra progressed during the twentieth century, so the use of vibrato increased. But, in Mendelssohn's day and before, orchestral vibrato was less of an issue. Performances were vibrato-less, and today many specialist players and orchestras have been learning, with greater and greater success, how to recreate the original sound. Though some listeners regret the loss of a warm bath of vibrato-laden string tone, the compensations in terms of incisiveness and authenticity are manifest. Besides, vibrato-lovers continue to be lavishly catered for by symphony orchestras which perform in the old familiar way.

**Vivace**. Italian term for 'lively'.